Leandro Gonzáles Moya
9-39-78-52

CROSSROADS 2

STUDENT BOOK

Shirley A. Brod
Irene Frankel

with

Earl W. Stevick

and

Spring Institute for International Studies

Oxford University Press

Oxford University Press

200 Madison Avenue
New York, NY 10016 USA

Walton Street
Oxford OX2 6DP England

OXFORD is a trademark of Oxford University Press.

Library of Congress Cataloging-in-Publication Data

Brod, Shirley A.
  Crossroads 2: student book / Shirley A. Brod, Irene Frankel, with
Earl W. Stevick and Spring Institute for International Studies.
    p. cm.
  ISBN 0-19-434381-2
  1. English language — Textbooks for foreign speakers. I. Frankel,
Irene. II. Stevick, Earl W.   III. Spring Institute for International Studies.
IV. Title. V. Title: Crossroads two.
PE1128.B679   1992   91–42779
428.2′4 — dc20   CIP

ISBN 0-19-434381-2

Editorial Manager: Susan Lanzano
Senior Editor: Ellen Lehrburger
Editor: John Sturtevant
Associate Editor: Paul Phillips
Design Manager: Lynn Luchetti
Designer: Maj-Britt Hagsted
Art Buyer/Picture Researcher: Karen Polyak, Paula Radding
Production Controller: Abram Hall

Cover illustration by Dennis Ziemienski

Continuing characters illustrated by Bob Marstall. Other interior
illustrations by Kathie Abrams, Abby Carter, Susan Detrich, Eldon Doty,
Tom Garcia, Gerry Gersten, Patrick Girouard, Laura Maestro, M. Chandler
Martylewski, Burton Morris, Steve Schindler, and Andrew Shiff.

Graphics, handwriting, and realia by Alan Barnett, Maj-Britt Hagsted,
Sharon Hudak, April Okano, and Stephan Van Litsenborg.

Printing (last digit): 10 9 8 7 6 5 4

Printed in Hong Kong

Acknowledgments

Thanks to the reviewers and consultants who helped to shape this book:

Fiona Armstrong, New York City Board of Education, New York, New York

Martha F. Burns, North Hollywood Adult Learning Center, North Hollywood, California

Ann Creighton, Los Angeles Unified School District, Los Angeles, California

Rheta Goldman, Los Angeles Unified School District, Los Angeles, California

Cliff Meyers, University of Massachusetts, Amherst, Massachusetts

Kathleen Santopietro, Colorado Department of Education, Denver, Colorado

Jack Wigfield, Alemany Campus, City College of San Francisco, San Francisco, California

We'd like to thank Oxford University Press for doing so much to facilitate our long-distance collaboration. We also like to thank our editors: Susan Lanzano, for so lovingly nurturing this project; Ellen Lehrburger, for guiding us through the process; Jane Sturtevant, for making everything work so well; and Paul Phillips, for paying attention to the details. Thanks, too, to everyone else at Oxford, especially Jim O'Connor.

Thanks to those from whom we've learned so much about teaching ESL and teaching adults: Virginia French Allen, James Asher, Charles Curran, John Fanselow, Caleb Gattegno, Autumn Keltner, Stephen Krashen, Harvey Nadler, Liz Steinberg, and Earl Stevick.

Thanks to Margot Gramer and Jenny Rardin for their unique contributions to this series.

Thanks to Myrna Ann Adkins and Barbara Sample of the Spring Institute for International Studies for making it possible for us to work together, and for supporting us in so many ways.

This book is dedicated to our husbands, Jerry Brod and David Martin, whose patience, flexibility, and support made all the difference; to Shirley's mother, Nell Brabham, for a lifetime of encouraging her to reach beyond the easy grasp; and to Irene's grandmother, Celia Levine, for introducing her to English as a second language.

Contents

	COMPETENCIES	GRAMMAR
UNIT 6 **Food** Page 61	Offer to help someone and respond to offers of help. State likes and dislikes. Ask for clarification using basic question words. Read prices, weights and measures for food, and abbreviations.	count and noncount nouns *some, any, much, many, a lot of* *how much, how many*

UNIT 7
Finding a Job
 	
Page 73
	Ask about job openings, set a time for a job interview, and
	    answer questions about work experience, work shifts,
	    starting date, and hours.
	Fill out a simple job application form.
		past tense of *be*
		can, can't

UNIT 8 **On the Job** Page 85	Follow oral instructions about where to put things. State need for tools. Give simple excuses for lateness or absence. Apologize for forgetting something. Ask to cash a check or money order and show proper ID. Endorse a check.	object pronouns *me, him,* etc. past tense of *be* *at, under* (location)

UNIT 9
Clothing
 	
Page 97
	Name common articles of clothing and ask for the size you
	    need.
	Respond to questions about payment.
	Identify incorrect change and ask for the right amount.
	Give simple descriptions of people.
	Read sizes and prices on tags.
		descriptive adjectives
		adjective comparisons
		    (*-er than*)

UNIT 10
Transportation
 	
Page 109
	Ask and answer questions about fares and departure and
	    arrival times, and buy travel tickets.
	Give information about the trip from your home country to
	    the United States.
	Read common traffic and pedestrian signs, and departure
	    and arrival schedules.
		always, usually, sometimes,
		    hardly ever, never

Grammar Summaries Page 121		
Tapescript for Listening Plus Page 124		
Basic Conversations for Progress Checks Page 131		
Useful Irregular Verbs Page 133		

To the Teacher

Crossroads

- is a four-level adult series in English as a second language
- integrates a competency-based approach with systematic grammar presentation
- covers the four skills of listening, speaking, reading, and writing
- is for adults and young adults in adult education or continuing education, or secondary programs
- begins lower and progresses more gradually than other beginning series
- provides an exceptionally complete and flexible array of classwork, homework, and teacher support materials through the Student Book, the Teacher's Book, the Multilevel Activity and Resource Package, the Workbook, and Cassettes.

Level 2

The **Student Book** has ten units with the following sections:

Getting Started	provides a context for new material
Conversations	new competencies, grammar and vocabulary
Paperwork	document literacy
Reading and Writing	literacy skills
Listening Plus	listening skills
Interactions	information gap
Progress Checks	demonstration of competency

The **Teacher's Book** provides:

- warm-up activities
- step-by-step procedures for each exercise
- suggestions for varying and extending the exercises
- ways to teach pronunciation
- cross-cultural and linguistic notes
- reproducible versions of unit opener illustrations
- reproducible Competency Checklists

The **Multilevel Activity and Resource Package** is reproducible and includes:

- listening, grammar, and writing worksheets in two versions, for multilevel classes
- handwriting worksheets
- word cards, picture cards, game boards, and maps, all with activities
- practical teaching notes

The **Workbook** is designed for independent study and homework. It contains:

- grammar and writing worksheets in two versions, for multilevel classes
- games, crossword puzzles, and word searches
- answer key

Practice conversations, Listening Plus, and reading texts are recorded on the **Cassettes.**

Placement

Place students in CROSSROADS 1 if they function minimally or not at all in English.

Place students in CROSSROADS 2 if they are able to function in a very limited way, depending largely on learned phrases.

Place students in CROSSROADS 3 if they have moved beyond a limited range of learned phrases and are beginning to function with some independence and creativity, but still have difficulty communicating even with someone who is used to dealing with people of limited English proficiency.

Place students in CROSSROADS 4 if they can communicate, although with some difficulty, on familiar topics with native speakers who are *not* accustomed to dealing with people of limited English proficiency.

CROSSROADS is compatible with the Comprehensive Adult Student Assessment System (CASAS) and the Student Performance Levels (SPL's) recommended by the Mainstream English Language Training (MELT) Project of the U.S. Department of Health and Human Services. SPL's are correlated with scores on the Basic English Skills Test (BEST).

	MELT SPL's	BEST Scores	CASAS Achievements Scores
CROSSROADS 1	I and II	9–28	165–190
CROSSROADS 2	III	29–41	191–196
CROSSROADS 3	IV and V	42–57	197–210
CROSSROADS 4	VI and VII	58–65+	211–224

Placement can also be made according to students' control of grammar. CROSSROADS 1 covers the present tense of *be*, the present continuous tense, and the simple present tense. CROSSROADS 2 covers the past tense of *be* and other verbs, and the future with *be going to*. CROSSROADS 3 covers the past tense with irregular verbs, the future tense with *will*, and the past progressive tense. CROSSROADS 4 covers the present perfect and present perfect continuous tenses.

One of these symbols in the margin next to an exercise tells you that a specific competency is first practiced there. In the Progress Checks pages, the same letter identifies the exercise that tests that competency.

Teaching Procedures

An underlying principle of CROSSROADS is *elicit before you teach.* Even at level two, before students tackle print, we suggest that they guess what the text might say, share any language they already know about the topic, listen to the text on cassette or read by their teacher, and learn or review key vocabulary. Similarly, before attempting independent pair practice, students might repeat the exercise aloud together, learn needed vocabulary, and participate in supervised pair practice.

Most instruction lines recur throughout the book and stand for, rather than spell out, complete teaching procedures. **Step-by-Step Teaching Procedures** for these recurring exercises appear on pages viii–ix, following this introduction. They state the purpose of the exercise and include preparation and follow-up steps to help students progress at their own pace, and to make written materials accessible to students with limited literacy skills.

Most exercises are covered by the Step-by-Step Teaching Procedures. Those that are not are covered in the Teacher's Book, which provides an individually tailored procedure for every Student Book exercise.

Many of the exercises in CROSSROADS ask students to provide information about themselves. Most students enjoy this and feel that it helps them learn. However, there may be times when students are unwilling or unable to supply personal information. Therefore, some of the teaching procedures suggest that students may provide fictitious rather than true information.

Progress Checks

The last two pages of each unit are Progress Checks, which allow you and the students to find out how well they have mastered the competencies presented in the unit. Even if your program is not competency-based, these exercises provide a useful way for students to demonstrate that they have acquired the language taught in the unit.

Each exercise tests a specific competency or competencies, identified by letter and by name. You can evaluate students yourself, have peers evaluate each other, or have students evaluate themselves. Reproducible Competency Checklists in the back of the Teacher's Book can help with record keeping.

The two-part exercises called *What are the people saying?/Do it yourself* allow students to demonstrate spoken competencies. In *What are the people saying?*, students work in pairs or alone to generate a conversation based on what they have practiced in the unit. They are prompted by pictures, and some of the words and sentences may be supplied. This first part of the exercise provides a review of what students have practiced, and also lets them demonstrate how well they control the grammatical structures involved. *What are the people saying?* can be done just orally, or followed up with writing. An answer key for *What are the people saying?*, Basic Conversations, appears in the back of the Student Book. The second part of the exercise, *Do it yourself,* is where competency is demonstrated.

When a competency requires reading *(Read the names of common medicines),* the needed reading material is provided in the exercise. Progress Checks are designed for classroom use, but most competencies are actually needed outside of the classroom, in the community. For this reason, *Do it yourself* sometimes involves a degree of role play and imagination. For example, to demonstrate the competency *Follow simple instructions for medical treatment,* "patients" mime what "doctors" tell them to do.

Culminating Activities

Each unit of Student Book 2 ends with a *Memo to the Teacher,* which suggests an activity to help students integrate their newly acquired competencies into their lives outside the classroom. These activities encourage students to draw upon all of their communicative resources and to exercise their creativity.

The *Memo* is not an evaluation tool like other exercises on the Progress Checks pages. It provides an opportunity for the students to bring their new language skills to bear on a fairly complex and extended task. Success is in completion of the task, rather than in accurate production of language.

Grammar Summary, Tapescript, Useful Irregular Verbs

These three sections, together with the Basic Conversations mentioned above, are located in the back of the Student Book.

The Grammar Summary presents complete paradigms of grammatical structures practiced in the Student Book, including those highlighted in *Focus on grammar* exercises. The Tapescript for Listening Plus lets you preview exercises and to read them aloud if the Cassette is not available. Useful Irregular Verbs includes 95 of the most frequently used irregular verbs in their base and past tense forms.

Step-by-Step Teaching Procedures
(in alphabetical order)

Fill in the form.

Gives practice in reading and filling in forms.

Note: Students may want or need to give fictitious information about themselves. Show that this is acceptable by repeating Step 2, giving obviously fictitious information about yourself.

1. Reproduce the blank form on the board or use an overhead projector.
2. Fill in the form one blank at a time with information about yourself. After filling in each blank, make a statement about yourself with the information you have just written.
3. Erase your information. Interview a volunteer and fill in the form again. Leave the filled-in form on the board for students to use as a model.
4. Have students fill in the forms in their books with their own information and check each other's work in pairs.

Focus on grammar.

Helps students infer grammatical principles without using grammar terms.

1. Choose a pair of items that contrast *(Where is the book?/Where are the books?)* Write the pair side by side on the board or overhead projector.
2. Read the two items aloud and have students repeat.
3. Provide another example like the left-hand item *(Where is the chair?),* write it underneath, and have students repeat.
4. Elicit the corresponding item for the right-hand column *(Where are the chairs?),* write it, and have students repeat.
5. Point to the next space in the right-hand column and elicit an example to fill it.
6. Elicit the corresponding item for the left-hand column.
7. Have students copy the items on a separate piece of paper.
8. Use the same procedure for the other contrasting pairs in the exercise.

Get information/Give information.

Provides an information gap for communicative practice of grammar and vocabulary.

1. Write the conversation on the board or use an overhead projector. Don't fill in the handwritten parts yet.

2. Review vocabulary students will be using in the exercise.
3. Show students that there are two pages. Divide the class into a Student A group and a Student B group. Have them open their books to the appropriate page.
4. Show students where A and B get their information and where to write their answers.
5. In the conversation on the board, fill in the blanks as in the example and read the conversation aloud.
6. Call on a volunteer from each group to say the conversation for the class.
7. Erase the information in the blanks. Call on other volunteers to say the conversation using the next cue. Fill in the blanks.
8. Have A's work with B's in pairs to do the exercises and fill in the information. Each student should change roles and do both pages.
9. Go over the answers with the whole class.

Guess.

Provides a context for the unit.

1. Give students a little time to look at the picture.
2. Have students identify the characters, or identify them yourself.
3. Ask where the characters are.
4. Ask students to guess what the characters are saying. All responses are valid here.
5. Respond to each guess by restating it in acceptable English.

Interview three classmates.

Provides communicative practice.

Note: Students may want or need to give fictitious information about themselves. Show that this is acceptable by repeating Step 2, giving obviously fictitious information about yourself.

1. Copy the questions on the board or overhead projector. Don't fill in the answers yet.
2. Invite a student to speak for the person whose information is given as the example in the book. Interview the volunteer and fill in the answers with students' help.
3. Say the interview questions one at a time and have students repeat them.
4. Erase the answers. Invite a student to interview you and write your answers on the board.

5. Correct the answers with the whole class.
6. Have students ask three classmates the questions and write their answers.

Practice. *(the first conversation in the unit)*

Introduces specific competencies, grammar, and/or vocabulary.
1. Play the tape or read the conversation aloud while students follow along silently in their books.
2. Use the pictures on the previous page or otherwise elicit or demonstrate the meaning of key words and phrases.
3. Have students repeat the conversation chorally and then practice in pairs.

Practice. *(after the first one in the unit)*

Introduces specific competencies, grammar, and/or vocabulary.
1. Give students a little time to look at the picture. Then have them close their books.
2. Encourage students to guess what the characters might be saying.
3. Play the tape or read the conversation aloud, indicating which character is speaking each line.
4. Have students say anything they can recall of the conversation. Acknowledge all contributions by restating them in acceptable English.
5. Play the tape or read the conversation aloud while students follow along silently in their books.
6. Elicit or demonstrate the meaning of key words and phrases.
7. Have students repeat the conversation chorally and then practice in pairs.

Read about _____.

Provides practice in reading prose.
1. Give students a few minutes to look at the story and read what they can.
2. Play the tape or read the story aloud while students follow silently in their books.
3. Play the tape or read the story one line at a time and have students repeat it chorally.
4. Ask volunteers to read single sentences aloud.

Read the form/bills/labels, etc.

Introduces vocabulary for these documents.
1. Draw an outline of the form or other document on the board or overhead projector.
2. Have students look at the form in their books and read aloud anything they can.
3. As each item is suggested, add it to the form on the board, say it, and have students repeat. Elicit or supply missing items.
4. Ask simple questions to check and confirm students' understanding of vocabulary. *(What's Antonio's phone number?* or *What's 684-9133?)*
5. Point to items in the form at random and have volunteers read them aloud.

6. Have students work in pairs to ask and answer questions like those in Step 4.

Read your story to your group.

Lets students share their writing.
1. Have a volunteer read her story aloud to the class. Lead the class in applause for the reader.
2. Have the class restate the story to confirm understanding. Encourage the volunteer to clarify meaning, if necessary.
3. Have students work in groups to read their stories in turn and to receive responses and applause from their peers.
4. Have students copy their stories on a separate piece of paper.
5. Publish the stories by posting them in the classroom.

Review...Write...Number.

Reviews and gives practice in writing unit vocabulary; gives practice in listening for specific information.
Note: Students hear conversations beyond the level they are expected to produce. They need only listen for specific information and for gist.

Review.

1. Check the tapescript in the back of the Student Book to find what vocabulary students need for the exercise.
2. Have students look at the illustrations and read or say anything they can about them. Acknowledge all contributions by repeating or restating in acceptable English.
3. When key vocabulary is suggested, write the item on the board or overhead projector, say it aloud, and have students repeat.
4. Point to items at random and have volunteers read them aloud.

Write.

1. Copy the answer blanks on the board or overhead projector.
2. Play the tape or read the first conversation aloud. Write the example on the board when students hear it.
3. Continue playing one conversation at a time and have students write their answers. Play the tape as many times as students need.
4. Have students compare their answers in pairs.
5. Play the tape again, one conversation at a time. Have a volunteer write the answers on the board. Correct the student's answers with the whole class.
6. Have students check their answers against the answers on the board, then play the tape once more so that students can verify their answers.

Number.

1. Play the tape or read the tapescript aloud one conversation at a time, as many times as students need. Have students number the illustrations in the order of the conversations they hear.
2. Have students compare their answers in pairs.
3. Play the tape again and have a volunteer write the answers on the board. Correct any errors with the whole class.
4. Have students check their answers against the answers on the board, then play the tape once more so that students can verify their answers.

Talk about _____.

Provides practice with competencies, grammar, and/or vocabulary.

1. Write the conversation on the board or overhead projector. Don't fill in the handwritten parts yet.
2. Show students where to get the information for the blanks and fill them in as in the example.
3. Read the conversation aloud and have students repeat.
4. Read the cues aloud one by one and have students repeat.
5. Have pairs of students say the conversation for the class until all the cues have been used.
6. Have students practice the conversation in pairs, changing partners, saying both parts, and using all the cues.

Talk about yourself.

Provides personalized practice with competencies, grammar, and vocabulary.

Note: Students may want or need to give fictitious information about themselves. Show that this is acceptable by repeating Step 3, giving obviously fictitious information about yourself.

1. Write the conversation on the board or overhead projector. Don't fill in the handwritten parts.
2. If there are cues, show students where to find them. Read them aloud one by one and have students repeat.
3. Fill in the blanks for yourself and a volunteer. Read the conversation aloud and have students repeat. Then have the volunteer say the conversation with you.
4. Fill in the conversation again with information about two more volunteers. Have the volunteers say the conversation for the class.
5. Have other pairs say the conversation for the class. If there are cues, use them all.
6. Have students practice in pairs, changing partners, saying both parts, and using all the cues.

What about you?

Gives practice in listening for gist and writing.

1. Play the tape once. Have students confer in groups to reconstruct the statement they heard. Circulate to hear what they say.
2. Repeat Step 1 until most groups have the gist of the statement.
3. Have each group say their reconstruction for the class. Approve those that capture the gist of the statement.
4. Play the tape again so that students can verify the reconstructions.
5. Have students answer the question on the tape by writing similar information about themselves. Circulate to give help and feedback.
6. Have several volunteers put their answers on the board. Correct any errors with the whole class.
7. Have students compare their own answers with the answers on the board, then check each other's answers in pairs.

What are the people saying?/Do it yourself.

Provides for demonstration of competency. See page vii, and in the Teacher's Book, page viii.

What are the people saying?

1. Have students work in pairs to identify the situation, the relationship of the people, and what the people are saying. Circulate to give help and feedback.
2. Have students work in two-pair groups to compare their answers and conversations.
3. Have volunteers act out the conversation for the class. Have the other students approve what they say or suggest changes.

Do it yourself.

1. Have students say the conversation with a partner, using their own information and/or whatever cues are supplied.
2. When a student has successfully demonstrated a competency, it can be checked off and dated or initialed.

What can you hear?

Prepares students to read the first conversation on the next page.

1. Have students look at the picture while you play the tape or read the tapescript aloud.
2. Have students volunteer any words or sentences they can recall from the conversation.
3. Acknowledge all contributions by restating them in acceptable English.
4. Let them hear the conversation again to elicit more pieces of it.

What can you say?

Introduces vocabulary.

1. Ask students to look at the picture(s) and say any words they can read or guess.
2. As each word is volunteered, write it on the board or overhead projector in a place corresponding to its location in the exercise.
3. Pronounce each word after you write it. Have students point to the word in their books and repeat it.
4. In the same way, add any words students have not volunteered.
5. Ask a volunteer to stand and hold up the book for the class to see. (In large classes, place several volunteers around the room.) Have seated volunteers say the words and have the student with the book point to the pictures.
6. Have students work in pairs, one saying a word and the other pointing.
7. Have students copy the words onto a separate piece of paper, practice writing each word several times, and then dictate the words to each other in pairs.

What can you say about _____ ?

Prepares students for the reading which follows.

1. Have students look at the illustration and say anything they can about it.
2. As each key word, phrase, or sentence is suggested, write it on the board or overhead projector. Say the item and have students repeat.
3. Add any key words, phrases or sentences from the reading that students have not volunteered.
4. Point to items on the board at random and have students read them aloud.

What's next?

Gives practice in using (a) social and (b) grammatical clues to meaning.

1. With students' books closed, write the first response for *a* on the board or overhead projector. Read it aloud and have students repeat.
2. Have students work in pairs to guess what might come before.
3. Have pairs volunteer their guesses. Help the class evaluate each guess.
4. Do the same with the other responses in *a*. Leave the responses on the board.
5. Have students open their books and have a volunteer come to the board.
6. Play the tape or read the tapescript aloud one conversation at a time. Have students point to the correct response in their books and have the volunteer point to it at the board. Play the tape as many times as students need to resolve disagreement.
7. Repeat the process for *b*.

Write about yourself.

Gives practice in more extended writing.

Note: Students may want or need to give fictitious information about themselves. Show that this is acceptable by repeating Steps 1 and 3, giving obviously fictitious information about yourself.

1. Tell your own story to the class, using the story in the book as a model.
2. Help students restate what you have said to confirm their understanding. *(You were born in Chicago.)*
3. Write your story on the board or overhead projector. Leave it for students to use as a model for their own writing.
4. Have students work in pairs and tell their stories to each other. After one student talks, the other student restates the story to confirm understanding.
5. Have students write their own stories. Encourage them to help each other. Circulate to give help as needed.

The Class Picnic

Introductions

Getting Started

1. **Guess. Where are Donna and Gloria? What are they saying?**

2. **What can you hear?**

Conversations

1. Practice.

Donna: Hi. I'm Donna Jones.
Gloria: Hello. My name is Gloria Rivas.
Donna: Glad to meet you, Gloria.
Gloria: Glad to meet you, too.

a

2. Talk about yourself. Meet five classmates.

A: Hello. My name is _____ .   OR   Hi. I'm _____ .

B: Hello. I'm _____ .   OR   Hi. My name is _____ .

A: Glad to meet you, _____ .

B: Glad to meet you, too.

3. Practice.

Gloria: Hi, Sue.
Sue: Oh, Gloria. Hi. Gloria, this is my husband, Van.
        Van, this is my friend, Gloria Rivas.
Van: Nice to meet you, Gloria.
Gloria: Nice to meet you, too.

b

4. Introduce two classmates.

A: _____ , this is _____ .

    _____ , this is _____ .

B: Nice to meet you, _____ .

C: Nice to meet you, too.

Conversations

5. Practice.

Van: Are you a new student, Antonio?
Antonio: Yes, I am. My wife is a new student, too.
Van: That's nice. Is she here tonight?
Antonio: No, she's not.
Van: What's her name?
Antonio: Elena.
Van: Where are you and your wife from, Antonio?
Antonio: We're from Mexico.

6. Focus on grammar. Review.

I	am	from Mexico.
They	are	
She	is	

My	friend is from Vietnam.
Your	
Our	
Their	
His	
Her	

7. Talk about the students.

A: ___What's his name___?

B: ___His name is Ahmed___.

A: Where ___is he___ from?

B: ___He's___ from ___Afghanistan___.

Ahmed
Afghanistan

Gloria
El Salvador

Antonio and Elena
Mexico

Donna
the United States

Sue and Van
Vietnam

Conversations

8. Talk about yourself.

A: What's your name?

B: _____.

A: Where are you from?

B: _____.

9. Introduce your partner to the class.

10. Practice.

Sue: Good night, Gloria.
Gloria: Oh, wait, Sue. Here are my new address and phone number.
Sue: Great. Thanks. See you Tuesday.
Gloria: OK. See you.

11. Say goodbye.

Paperwork

1. **Read Sue's address book.**

NAME - ADDRESS			PHONE
NAME Antonio Medina			AREA CODE 209
ADDRESS 7886 Westside Dr.		APT. 5	PHONE 684-9133
CITY Bridgeton	STATE CA	ZIP CODE 93204	
NAME			AREA CODE
ADDRESS		APT.	PHONE
CITY	STATE	ZIP CODE	
NAME			AREA CODE
ADDRESS		APT.	PHONE
CITY	STATE	ZIP CODE	
NAME			AREA CODE
ADDRESS		APT.	PHONE
CITY	STATE	ZIP CODE	

2. **Write your address and phone number in Sue's address book.**

3. **Practice.**

Sue: Could you spell your name, please?
Antonio: My first name or my last name?
Sue: Your last name.
Antonio: M-E-D-I-N-A.
Sue: And what's your address?
Antonio: 7886 Westside Drive, Apartment 5, Bridgeton.
Sue: 7886 Westside Drive. What's the ZIP code?
Antonio: It's 93204.
Sue: And what's your phone number?
Antonio: (209) 684-9133.
Sue: OK. Thanks.

4. **Interview three classmates. Make your own address book.**
   Use the conversations in 3.

Reading and Writing _____

1. What can you say about Young Ho Kim?

```
┌─────────────────────────────────────────────────┐
│          Student Information                      │
│  WESTSIDE COMMUNITY ADULT SCHOOL                  │
│                                                   │
│   Name: Young Ho Kim                              │
│   Address: 8324 Second Ave.    Apt. 6A            │
│   City: Bridgeton  State: CA  ZIP Code: 93201     │
│   Area Code: 209  Phone: 338-7212                 │
│   Country of Origin: Korea                        │
│   First Language: Korean                          │
└─────────────────────────────────────────────────┘
```

2. Read about Young Ho.

    My name is Young Ho Kim. I'm from Korea. I'm a student at the Westside Community Adult School. My first language is Korean. I speak a little English.

3. Write about Young Ho.

    His name is Young Ho Kim. _____

_____

_____

_____

_____

4. Write your story. Fill in the blanks. Use Young Ho's story as an example.

    My name is _____. I'm from _____. I'm a student at _____. My first language is _____. I speak a little English.

5. Copy your story on a separate piece of paper.

6. Read your story to your group.

6

Reading and Writing _____

7. What can you say about Sue's class?

8. Read about Sue's class.

  I'm in the ESL 2 class at the Westside Community Adult School. There are eight students, four men and four women. We're from six different countries, and we speak four different languages. We all speak a little English.

9. Work in pairs. Fill in the chart.

	Sue's Class	Your Class
Name of class	ESL 2	
Name of school		
Number of students		
Number of men		
Number of women		
Number of countries		
Number of languages		

**10. Write about your class. Use a separate piece of paper.
Use the story in 8 as an example.**

Listening Plus

1. What's next?

    a. That's nice.   Nice to meet you.   Good night.

    b. Yes, I am.   No, he's not.   Yes, they are.

2. Review...Write...Number.

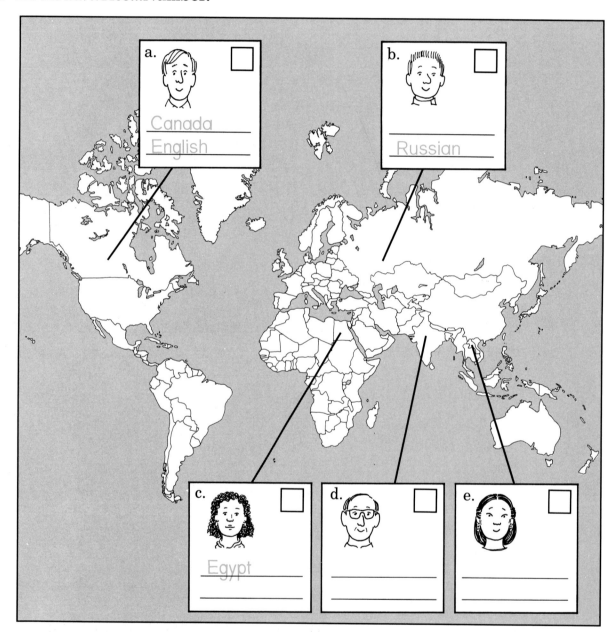

a. Canada / English

b. Russian

c. Egypt

d.

e.

3. A, tell about a person in 2. B, say what you heard and point.

4. What about you?

Interactions _____

Student A

1. **Get information. Ask about the words for your boxes.**

    A: What's in Box __C__?

    B: ___Books___ .

    A: How do you spell that?

    B: ___B-O-O-K-S___ .

    A: Excuse me?

    B: ___B-O-O-K-S___ .

    A: ___B-O-O-K-S. Books___ . Thanks.

C	D	E
_____books_____	clocks	_____
F	**G**	**H**
chalk	_____	pencils
I	**J**	**K**
_____	a notebook	_____
L	**M**	**N**
a window	_____	books

2. **Give information. Tell about the pictures on your page.**

Interactions

Student B

1. **Give information. Tell about the pictures on your page.**

   A: What's in Box __C__ ?

   B: ___Books___ .

   A: How do you spell that?

   B: ___B-O-O-K-S___ .

   A: Excuse me?

   B: ___B-O-O-K-S___ .

   A: ___B-O-O-K-S. Books___ . Thanks.

C	D	E
books	_____	a door
F	G	H
_____	a shelf	_____
I	J	K
pens	_____	a chalkboard
L	M	N
_____	pencils	_____

2. **Get information. Ask about words for your boxes.**

Progress Checks ✔

1. e ☐ Fill in a simple form, including name, address,
           phone number and area code.
    i ☐ Write your country of origin.
    j ☐ Write your first language.

Fill in the form.

STUDENT INFORMATION CARD

Name: _____

Area Code: _____ Phone: _____

Address: _____ Apt. _____

City: _____ State: _____ ZIP Code: _____

Country of Origin: _____

First Language: _____

---

2. h ☐ State your address, phone number, and area code.

Ask questions. Fill in the form for a classmate.

STUDENT INFORMATION CARD

Name: _____

Area Code: _____ Phone: _____

Address: _____ Apt. _____

City: _____ State: _____ ZIP Code: _____

---

3. f ☐ Ask someone to spell something.
    g ☐ Spell something aloud.

What are the people saying?

Do it yourself.

Progress Checks

4.
- a ☐ Introduce yourself.
- b ☐ Introduce others.
- c ☐ Say where you are from.
- d ☐ Say goodbye.

What are the people saying?

Do it yourself.

❖❖❖ **Memo** ❖❖❖

TO: the teacher

Have students choose new identities (of friends, family members, famous people). Have them introduce themselves in pairs. Then have them introduce each other to another pair of students. Encourage them to extend their conversations as much as they can.

2 Housing

Getting Started _____

1. **Guess. Where are Antonio, Elena, and the apartment manager?
   What are they saying?**

2. **What can you hear?**

Conversations

1. Practice.

Antonio: Hello. We're looking for an apartment.
Gina: Please come in. I'm Gina Lombardo.
Antonio: How do you do? I'm Antonio Medina. This is my wife, Elena.
Elena: Nice to meet you, Ms. Lombardo.
Gina: Nice to meet you, too. Have a seat, please.
Antonio: Thanks.

2. Talk about yourself.

A: I'm _____.

B: How do you do? I'm _____.

A: Nice to meet you, _____.

3. What can you say?

a furnished room

a house

an apartment

4. Practice.

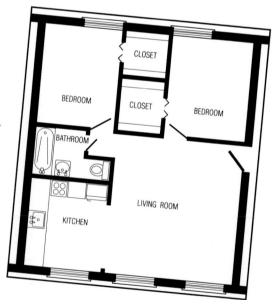

Antonio: Do you have an apartment for rent?
Gina: Yes, I do. It's a very nice apartment.
Elena: How many rooms does it have?
Gina: Four rooms. Two bedrooms with big closets, a kitchen, and a living room.
Elena: Oh, good. We need two bedrooms.
Antonio: What's the rent?
Gina: $700.
Antonio: And what's the deposit?
Gina: $1,400.

Conversations _____

a
b

5. Talk about rooms, rents, and deposits. Use your imagination.

A: How many rooms does the apartment have?

B: It has ___three_____ rooms, _a bedroom, a living room, and a kitchen_.

A: What's the rent, please?

B: ___$650_____.

A: And what's the deposit?

B: ___$1,300_____.

6. What can you say?

UTILITIES		
water	gas	electricity

7. Practice.

Antonio: Does the rent include utilities?
Gina: It includes water.
Antonio: What about electricity?
Gina: No, it doesn't include electricity or gas.
            They're extra.

8. Focus on grammar. Review.

They	need	an apartment.
He	needs	

They	don't	need a big kitchen.
He	doesn't	

Do	they	need two bedrooms?
Does he		

Yes,	they	do.
	he	does.

No,	they	don't.
	he	doesn't.

c

9. Talk about yourself. Use the words in 6.

A: Does your rent include utilities?

B: It includes _water, but it doesn't include gas and electricity_.

Unit 2   15

Conversations

10. What can you say?

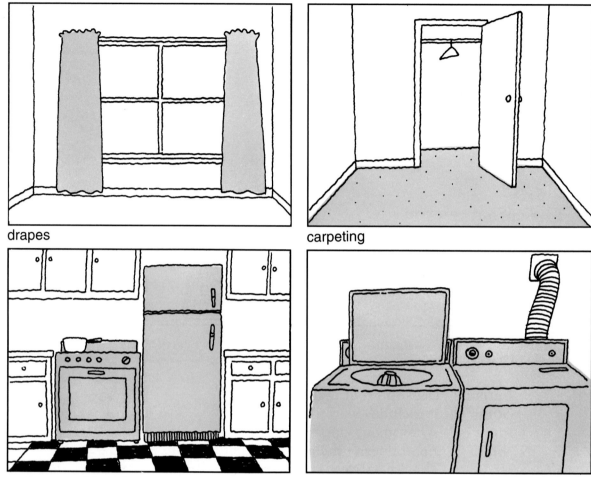

drapes

carpeting

a stove, a refrigerator

a washer, a dryer

11. Practice.

Elena: Is the apartment furnished?
Gina: No, it's unfurnished. But it has a stove and refrigerator.
Antonio: Does it have drapes and carpeting?
Gina: It has carpeting, but it doesn't have drapes.
Elena: What about a washer and dryer?
Gina: There's a laundry room next to the office with new washers
           and dryers.

d **12. Talk about a house or apartment. Use the words in 10.
Use your imagination.**

A: Does the ___apartment___ have ___drapes___?

B: ___No, it doesn't, but it has carpeting___.

Paperwork

1. Read Ahmed's utility bills for September.

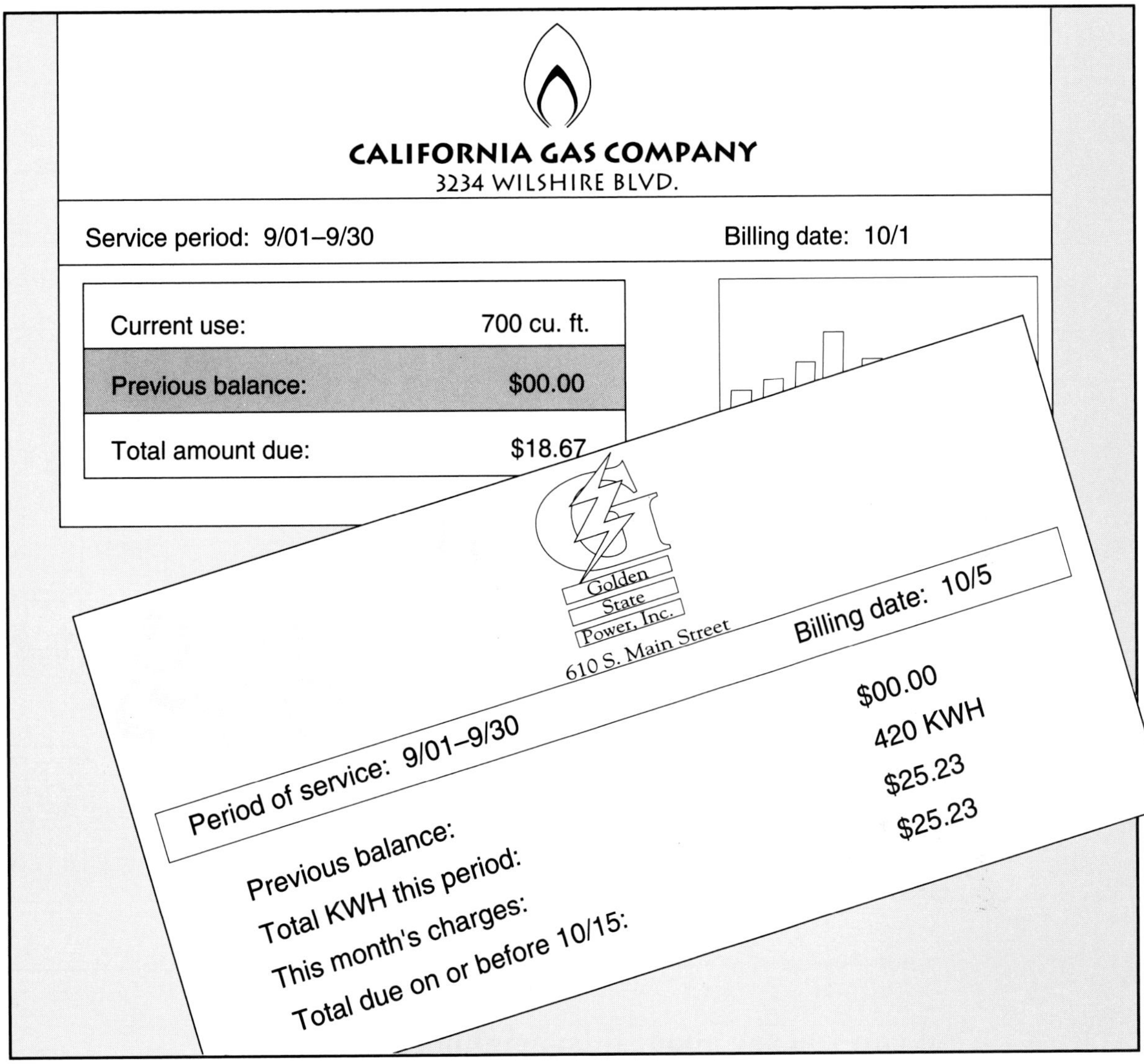

CALIFORNIA GAS COMPANY
3234 WILSHIRE BLVD.

Service period: 9/01–9/30 — Billing date: 10/1

Current use:	700 cu. ft.
Previous balance:	$00.00
Total amount due:	$18.67

Golden State Power, Inc.
610 S. Main Street

Period of service: 9/01–9/30 — Billing date: 10/5

Previous balance:	$00.00
Total KWH this period:	420 KWH
This month's charges:	$25.23
Total due on or before 10/15:	$25.23

e

2. How much is his gas bill this month? Circle the total due.
How much is his electric bill this month? Circle the amount.

3. Interview three classmates. Write their answers on a separate sheet of paper.

How much is your water bill? —

How much is your gas bill? $18.67

How much is your electric bill? $25.23

How much are your utility bills this month? $43.90

Reading and Writing _____

1. **This is Antonio and Elena's neighborhood. Label the picture.**
   Use these words:

   apartment house   clinic   supermarket   school

   hospital   park   bus stop

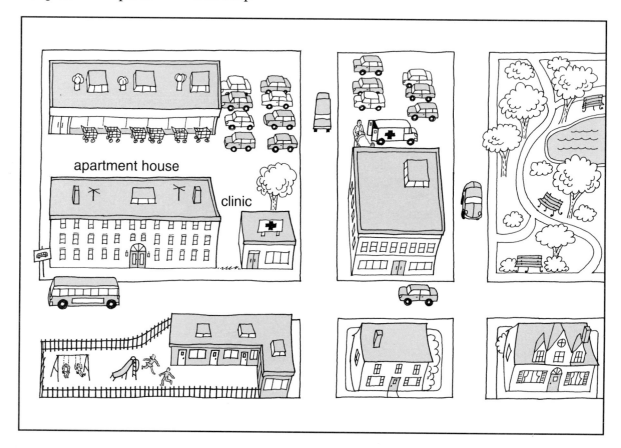

2. **What can you say about this neighborhood?**
   Use these words:

   across the street   down the block   on the corner

   two blocks away   around the corner   on the next block

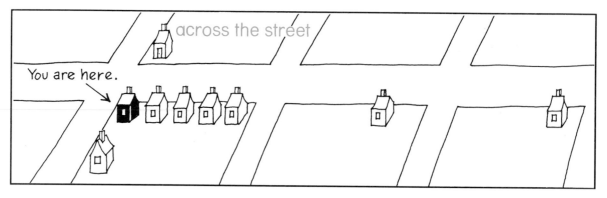

Reading and Writing _____

 3. **Read Elena's letter to her friend Sandy.**

September 4

Dear Sandy,
   Antonio and I have a new apartment. It has four rooms.
There are two bedrooms, a living room, and a kitchen. It's
on 12th Avenue.
   The children's school is across the street. There's a bus
stop on the corner and a clinic down the block. There's a
beautiful park two blocks away. The supermarket is around
the corner, and there's a hospital on the next block.
   Please visit soon.

Love,
Elena

4. **Draw a map of your neighborhood. Label the map. Use the map
in 1 as an example.**

5. **Write a letter about your neighborhood. Use a separate
piece of paper.**

6. **Read your letter to your group.**

Listening Plus

 1. What's next?

    a. How do you do?   Thanks.   It's very nice.

    b. Yes, they do.   No, I don't.   Yes, it does.

2. Review...Write...Number.

a.

Rent: _$685.00_

Deposit: _$1,027.50_

b.

Rent: _____

Deposit: _____

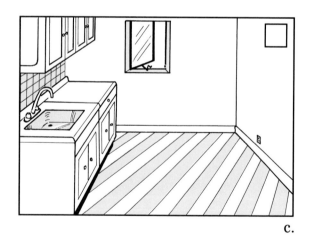

c.

Rent: _____

Deposit: _____

d.

Rent: _____

Deposit: _____

3. A, describe an apartment in 2. B, say what you heard and point.

4. What about you?

_____

Interactions

Student A

f 1. **Get information. Ask about these places near Gloria's apartment. Write the places on the map.**

    a. the police station   b. the bus stop   c. the supermarket

    d. the post office   e. the park   f. the bank

    A: Where's ___the police station___?

    B: It's ___on the corner___.

    A: ___Is it left or right___?

    B: ___Right___.

2. **Give information.**

Unit 2

21

Interactions _____

Student B

1. Give information.

A: Where's ___the police station___?

B: It's ___on the corner___.

A: ___Is it left or right___?

B: ___Right___.

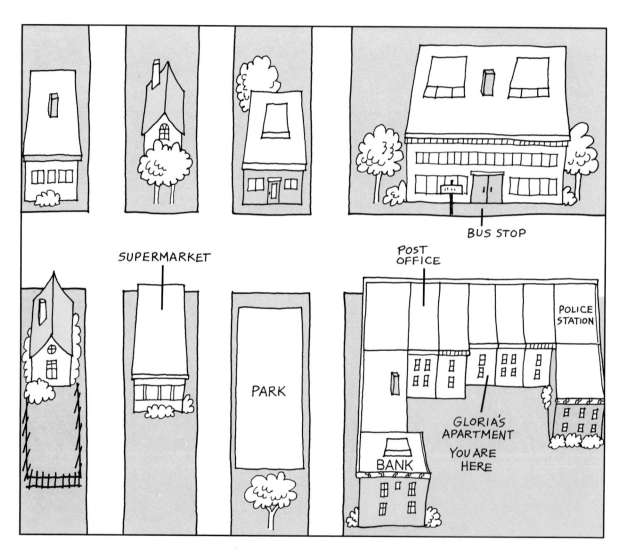

2. Get information. Ask about these places near Gloria's apartment. Write the places on the map.

a. the library   b. the fire station   c. the drugstore

d. the school   e. the hospital   f. the clinic

Progress Checks ✔

1. d ☐ Identify basic types of housing.
   b ☐ Ask about rent and deposits.
   c ☐ Find out about utilities.
   a ☐ Ask about the number and types of rooms.

What are the people saying?

Do it yourself.

2. f ☐ Ask for information about locations of places in a neighborhood.

What are the people saying?

Do it yourself.

Progress Checks

3. e ☐ Identify the total due on monthly bills.

Circle the total amount due.

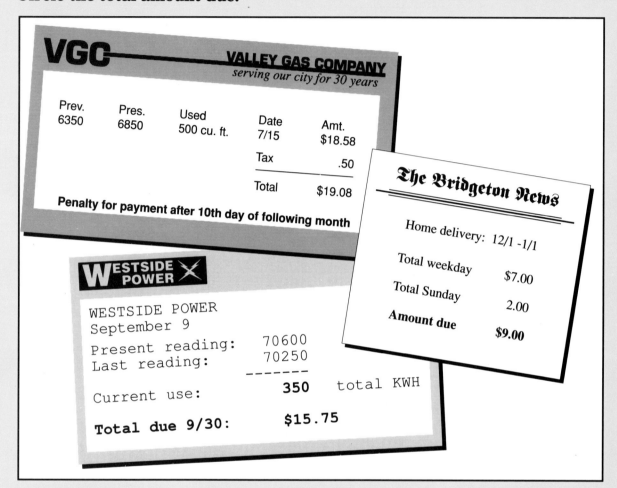

VGC — **VALLEY GAS COMPANY**
serving our city for 30 years

Prev. 6350	Pres. 6850	Used 500 cu. ft.	Date 7/15	Amt. $18.58
			Tax	.50
			Total	$19.08

Penalty for payment after 10th day of following month

The Bridgeton News

Home delivery: 12/1 -1/1

Total weekday	$7.00
Total Sunday	2.00
Amount due	**$9.00**

WESTSIDE POWER X

```
WESTSIDE POWER
September 9
Present reading:   70600
Last reading:      70250
                 --------
Current use:          350   total KWH

Total due 9/30:     $15.75
```

❖ ❖ ❖ **Memo** ❖ ❖ ❖

TO: the teacher
Have half of the students be apartment managers and the others be apartment hunters. Each manager has one apartment to rent. Managers help each other decide details about their apartments. Renters help each other decide what each is looking for (numbers of rooms, cost of rent and utilities, amount of deposit, community services, and stores). Renters then go around the classroom, and talk to different managers to find an apartment that meets their needs.

3 Community Services

Getting Started

1. Guess. Where are Gloria, Sue, and Van? What are they saying?

2. What can you hear?

Conversations _____

1. Practice.

Gloria: Hi, Sue. Hi, Van. What are you doing here?
Sue: I want to get my driver's license, but first I have to get my learner's permit.
Van: And I have to take my road test. What about you?
Gloria: I need to get an ID card. Good luck on your tests.
Van: Thanks.
Sue: Thanks, Gloria. See you in class tonight.

2. What can you say?

the written test

the eye test

the road test

an ID card

a change of address form

a learner's permit

3. Talk about going to the Department of Motor Vehicles. Use the words in 2.

A: Hi, _____.What are you doing here?

B: I have to _get my learner's permit_.

What about you?

A: I need to _take my road test_.

Conversations _____

4. Practice.

Gloria: Hi, Van. Did you pass your road test?
Van: Yes, I did.
Gloria: Congratulations!
Van: Thanks. Now I need to buy a car.
Gloria: What about Sue? Did she get her learner's permit?
Van: No, she didn't.
Gloria: Oh, that's too bad.

5. Focus on grammar.

Did	they she	pass the test?

Yes,	they she	did.

No,	they she	didn't.

6. Talk about the people.

A: Did ___he take his road test___?

B: ___Yes, he did___.

take his road test

buy a car

pass the written test

get a driver's license

pass the eye test

get her learner's permit

Conversations _____

7. Practice.

Gloria: Hi, Sue. How are you?
Sue: Not so good. I didn't get my learner's permit.
Gloria: Yes, I know. I'm sorry. Did you study?
Sue: Yes. I studied a lot. I passed the written test, but I didn't pass the eye test.
Gloria: What happened?
Sue: I need glasses.

8. Focus on grammar.

They	passed / didn't pass	the test.

pass	study	need
passed	studied	needed

They	took / didn't take	the test.

take	have	get
took	had	got

9. Talk about the people.

A: Did ___he pass the road test___?

B: ___No, he didn't pass the road test___.

pass the road test

take the eye test

study for the written test

need glasses

get his license

have her ID card

Paperwork _____

1. Read Gloria's application.

> **APPLICATION FOR IDENTIFICATION CARD (Print in ink.)**
>
> FULL NAME _____Gloria_____Estela_____Rivas_____
>   (First)   (Middle)   (Last)
>
> MAILING ADDRESS __7623 Union St._____ Apt. # _5__
>
> CITY _Bridgeton_____ STATE _CA___ ZIP CODE _93201_____
>
> SEX ☐ M ☑ F   COLOR HAIR ___black____ COLOR EYES ___brown____
>
> HEIGHT _5'3"_____ WEIGHT __120 lbs.___ DATE OF BIRTH ___4/8/62___
>   (Month/Day/Year)

2. Fill in the application. Choose from these words.

Hair color: brown   blond   red   black   gray   white

Eye color: brown   blue   gray   green   hazel

> **APPLICATION FOR IDENTIFICATION CARD (Print in ink.)**
>
> FULL NAME _____
>   (First)   (Middle)   (Last)
>
> MAILING ADDRESS _____ Apt. # _____
>
> CITY _____ STATE _____ ZIP CODE _____
>
> SEX ☐ M ☐ F   COLOR HAIR _____ COLOR EYES _____
>
> HEIGHT _____ WEIGHT _____ DATE OF BIRTH _____
>   (Month/Day/Year)

3. Interview three classmates. Write their answers on a separate piece of paper.

What color is your hair? __black_____

What color are your eyes? __brown_____

Do you have a picture ID card? __no_____

Do you have a driver's license? __no_____

Reading and Writing _____

1. What can you say about Antonio? Use these words:

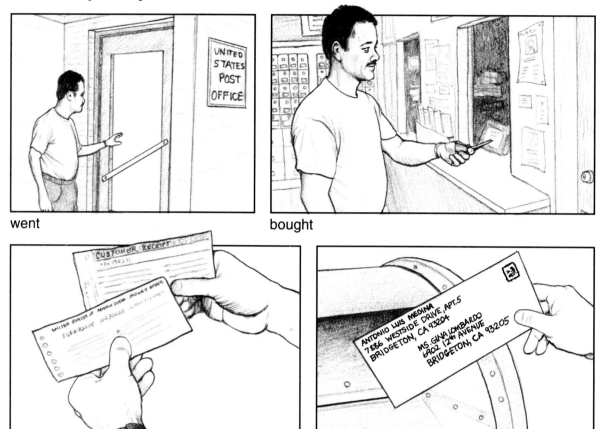

went

bought

filled out   kept

wrote   sent

2. Read about Antonio.

Antonio needed two money orders for the deposit on his new apartment. He went to the post office and bought the money orders. He filled out the money orders and kept the receipts. He wrote the address on the envelope and sent the money orders to Gina Lombardo, the apartment manager.

3. Number the sentences in order.

_____ He sent the money orders to the building manager.

_____ He kept the receipts.

_____ He bought two money orders.

_____ He filled out the money orders.

__1__ Antonio went to the post office.

_____ He wrote the address on the envelope.

Reading and Writing _____

4. **Send this money order to Barbara Day. Her address is 12743 Main St., Bridgeton, CA 93204.**

b   a. Fill out the money order.

c   b. Write the address on the envelope. Include your return address.

5. **Write about yourself. Fill in the blanks. Use the words in 1. Use Antonio's story as an example.**

I ____needed____ a money order for a deposit on a new apartment. I

_____ to the post office and _____ a money order for

$500. I _____ the money order and _____ the receipt.

I _____ the address on the envelope and _____ the

money order to Barbara Day.

6. **Copy your story on a separate piece of paper. Check your story with a classmate.**

Listening Plus

1. What's next?

    a. Congratulations.   Good luck.   That's too bad.

    b. Yes, they did.   No, she didn't.   Yes, he does.

2. Review...Write...Number.

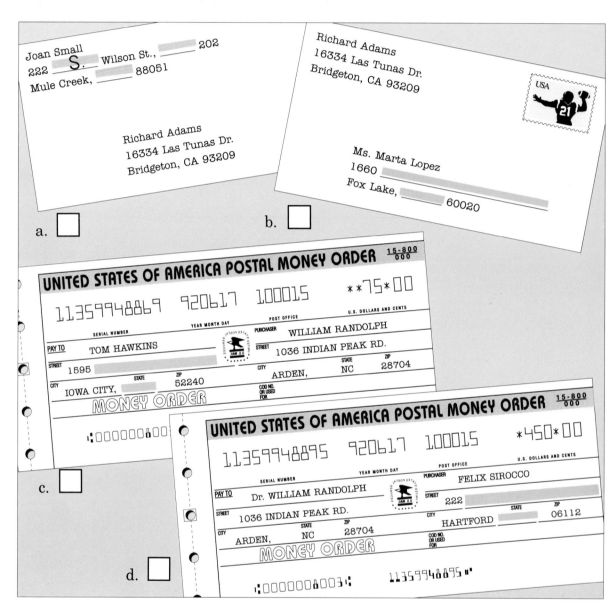

3. A, tell about a picture in 2. B, say what you heard and point.

4. What about you?

Interactions _____

Student A

1. **Get information about Ray. Continue the conversation.**
   Fill in the application.

   A: What's his middle name?
   B: Manuel.
   A: How do you spell that?
   B: M-A-N-U-E-L.

   ┌───┐
   │ **APPLICATION FOR DRIVER LICENSE (Print in ink.)**   │
   │   │
   │ FULL NAME _____ Ray _____ Manuel _____ Sanchez ____   │
   │   (First)   (Middle)   (Last)   │
   │ MAILING ADDRESS _____ Apt. # ____ │
   │   │
   │ CITY _____ STATE _____ ZIP CODE _____   │
   │   │
   │ SEX ☑ M ☐ F COLOR HAIR _____ COLOR EYES _____   │
   │   │
   │ HEIGHT _____ WEIGHT _____ DATE OF BIRTH _____ │
   │   (Month/Day/Year) │
   └───┘

2. **Give information about Donna.**

   ┌───┐
   │ **APPLICATION FOR DRIVER LICENSE (Print in ink.)**   │
   │   │
   │ FULL NAME _____ Donna _____ Ann _____ Jones ____   │
   │   (First)   (Middle)   (Last)   │
   │ MAILING ADDRESS _ 1400 Main St. _____ Apt. # ____ │
   │   │
   │ CITY _ Bridgeton _____ STATE __ CA __ ZIP CODE _ 93207 __ │
   │   │
   │ SEX ☐ M ☑ F COLOR HAIR ___ blond ___ COLOR EYES _ green __ │
   │   │
   │ HEIGHT _ 5'4" ___ WEIGHT _ 115 lbs. _ DATE OF BIRTH _ 12/11/28 _ │
   │   (Month/Day/Year) │
   └───┘

Interactions

Student B

1. **Give information about Ray.**

   A: What's his middle name?
   B: Manuel.
   A: How do you spell that?
   B: M-A-N-U-E-L.

   ### APPLICATION FOR DRIVER LICENSE (Print in ink.)

   FULL NAME _____ Ray _____ Manuel _____ Sanchez _____
                       (First)   (Middle)   (Last)

   MAILING ADDRESS 717 2nd Ave. _____ Apt. # 3F

   CITY Bridgeton _____ STATE CA ___ ZIP CODE 93208

   SEX ☑ M ☐ F COLOR HAIR gray _____ COLOR EYES hazel

   HEIGHT 5' 10" ____ WEIGHT 155 lbs. ___ DATE OF BIRTH ____ 7/4/48
                                                              (Month/Day/Year)

2. **Get information about Donna. Continue the conversation.**
   Fill in the application.

   ### APPLICATION FOR DRIVER LICENSE (Print in ink.)

   FULL NAME _____ Donna _____
                       (First)   (Middle)   (Last)

   MAILING ADDRESS _____ Apt. # ____

   CITY _____ STATE _____ ZIP CODE _____

   SEX ☐ M ☑ F COLOR HAIR _____ COLOR EYES _____

   HEIGHT _____ WEIGHT _____ DATE OF BIRTH _____
                                                                 (Month/Day/Year)

Progress Checks ✔

1. b ☐ Fill out a money order.

Fill out the money order. For *Pay to*, use a name and address you know.

2. c ☐ Correctly address an envelope including return address.

Address the envelope for the money order in 1.

Progress Checks ✔

3. a ☐ Fill out an application for a driver's license or I D.

Fill out the application.

APPLICATION FOR IDENTIFICATION CARD (Print in ink.)

FULL NAME _____
                    (First)   (Middle)   (Last)

                                              COLOR HAIR _____

Sex ☐ M ☐ F   COLOR EYES _____   WEIGHT _____

                                  HEIGHT _____

DATE OF BIRTH _____
                 (Month/Day/Year)   Apt.# _____

MAILING ADDRESS _____   ZIP CODE _____

CITY _____ STATE _____

❖ ❖ ❖ Memo ❖ ❖ ❖

TO: the teacher
Bring in real application forms for a driver's license or picture
ID card from the local Department of Motor Vehicles. Have
students fill out applications.

4 School

Getting Started _____

1. Guess. Where are Olga, Yuri, and Ray? What are Yuri and Ray saying?

2. What can you hear?

Conversations _____

1. **Practice.**

   Ray: Hello. May I help you?
   Yuri: Yes, please. This is my grandmother.
          She wants to enroll in school.
   Ray: Sure.

2. **What can you say?**

   Olga
   grandmother   grandparents   Boris
                                   grandfather

   Elena   Mikhail   Natalya   Vladimir
   aunt   uncle   mother   father
                                        parents

   Yuri   Ivan   Anna
                  brother   sister

3. **Talk about Yuri's family.**

   A: Who's __Olga_____?

   B: __Olga_____ is Yuri's __grandmother_____.

4. **Draw your family on a separate piece of paper.**
   Talk about your family.

   A: Who's that?

   B: That's my _____.

Conversations _____

5. Practice.

Ray:	OK. Let me see. When did you come to the United States?
Yuri:	We came here in 1990.
Olga:	Yes. On May 20, 1990.
Ray:	You speak English very well.
Olga:	Thank you.
Ray:	Where did you study English?
Olga:	I studied English in New York.
Yuri:	We lived in New York last year.

6. Focus on grammar.

Where did they	study English? go to school?

They	studied went to school	in New York.

When did he	enroll come	here?

He	enrolled came	here on May 20, 1990.

7. Talk about the people.

A: ___When___ did ___he come here___ ?

B: ___He came here on June 3, 1989___ .

a. When/come here?
on June 3, 1989

Where/study English?
in El Salvador

b. Where/go to school?
in Vietnam

When/enroll here?
in September

c. Where/live last year?
in California

When/pass her test?
last week

Conversations

8. Practice.

Ray: And when did you come to California?
Yuri: We came to California three months ago.
Ray: How long did you study English in New York?
Olga: I studied English for six months.
Ray: I see. And how long did you go to school in Russia?
Olga: I went to school there for nine years, but I didn't study English.

9. Focus on grammar.

When did you come to California?	Three weeks ago. Last week. On March 4. In May. In 1990.
How long did you live in New York?	For ten years.

10. Talk about Olga.

A: ___When___ did Olga ___come to the U.S.___?

B: She ___came to the U.S. in May 1990___.

a. When/come to the U.S.?
   May 1990

b. When/live in New York?
   last year

c. How long/go to school?
   nine years

d. How long/study English in Russia?
   didn't/in Russia

11. Talk about yourself. Use the questions in 10.

Paperwork

1. Read Olga's enrollment form.

ENROLLMENT FORM	WESTSIDE COMMUNITY ADULT SCHOOL

Name
Mr./Ms./(Mrs.)/Miss __Horowitz__ __Olga__ _____ Date ___3/4/92___
                      Last   First   Middle Initial   Mo.   Day   Year

Address __200 Jefferson St., Apt. B, Bridgeton, CA 93202__

Phone __(209)346-6213__   Marital Status: ☐ Single   ☑ Married
                                        ☐ Separated   ☐ Divorced   ☐ Widowed

Date of Birth __5/3/30__ Age __61__ Birthplace __Russia__

Language __Russian__   Date of Arrival in U.S. __5/20/90__

Number of Years of School __9__   Years of English Study __6 months__

In Case of Emergency Notify __Mikhail Horowitz__ __(209)346-6213__ __son__
                                              Name   Phone Number   Relationship

b   **2. Fill in the form. Use the date you enrolled in your adult school.**

ENROLLMENT FORM	WESTSIDE COMMUNITY ADULT SCHOOL

Name
Mr./Ms./Mrs./Miss _____ Date _____
                      Last   First   Middle Initial   Mo.   Day   Year

Address _____

Phone _____   Marital Status: ☐ Single   ☐ Married
                                        ☐ Separated   ☐ Divorced   ☐ Widowed

Date of Birth _____ Age _____ Birthplace _____

Language _____ Date of Arrival in U.S. _____

Number of Years of School _____ Years of English Study _____

In Case of Emergency Notify _____
                                              Name   Phone Number   Relationship

c   **3. Interview three classmates. Write their answers on a separate piece of paper.**

How long did you go to school? __9 years__

When did you arrive in the U.S.? __5/20/90__

When did you enroll in this school? __3/4/92__

Reading and Writing _____

1. What can you say about Ramona and her family?

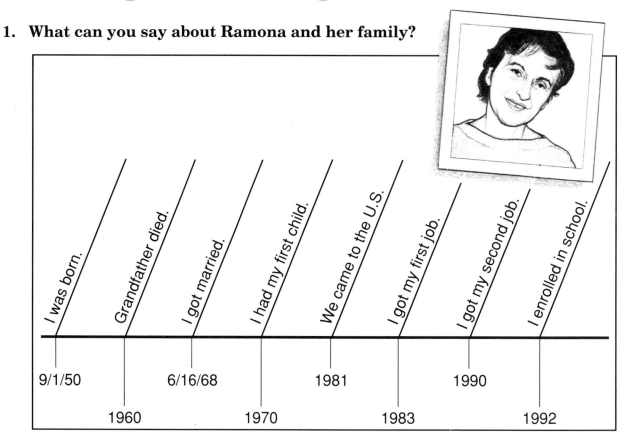

I was born.

Grandfather died.

I got married.

I had my first child.

We came to the U.S.

I got my first job.

I got my second job.

I enrolled in school.

| 9/1/50 | | 6/16/68 | | 1981 | | 1990 | |
| 1960 | | 1970 | | 1983 | | 1992 |

2. Read about Ramona and her family.

    I was born on September 1, 1950, in Guatemala City, Guatemala. I lived there with my grandfather, parents, three sisters, and four brothers. I went to school for five years. My grandfather died in 1960.

    I got married on June 16, 1968. I had my first child in 1970, my second child in 1972, and my third child in 1974.

    We came to the United States ten years ago. I got my first job in 1983, and I worked there for six years. I got my next job in 1990. Last year I enrolled in the Westside Community Adult School. Now I'm in the ESL 2 class.

3. Answer the questions on a separate piece of paper.

a. When was Ramona born? _Ramona was born on September 1, 1950_.
b. How long did she go to school in Guatemala?
c. When did Ramona's grandfather die?
d. When did she get married?
e. When did she have her children?
f. How long did she work in her first job?
g. When did she enroll in the adult school?
h. How old is Ramona?

Reading and Writing _____

d   4. **Fill in the form for your family. Include parents, brothers,
         sisters, husband or wife, and children.**

Name	Age	Relationship to You

5. **Write a time line for yourself and your family.**

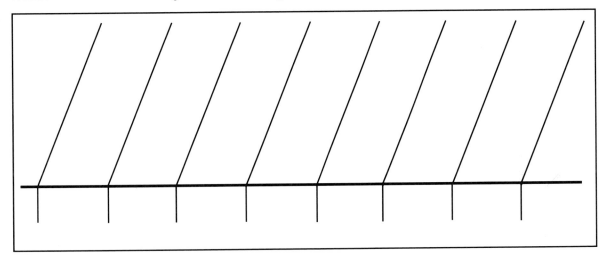

6. **Write about yourself. Use the story about Ramona and her
        family as an example.**

_____

_____

_____

_____

_____

7. **Read your story to your group.**

Listening Plus

 1. What's next?

    a. Eight months ago.   For one year.   It's July 9, 1982.

    b. No, they didn't.   Yes, she did.   No, he didn't.

2. Review...Write...Number.

3. A, tell about the people in 2. B, say what you heard and point.

 4. What about you?

Interactions

Student A

1. **Get information about Ovidio. Continue the conversation.**
    Fill in the form.

    A: When was Ovidio born?
    B: He was born on April 28, 1962.
    A: Did you say April 28, 1962?
    B: That's right.

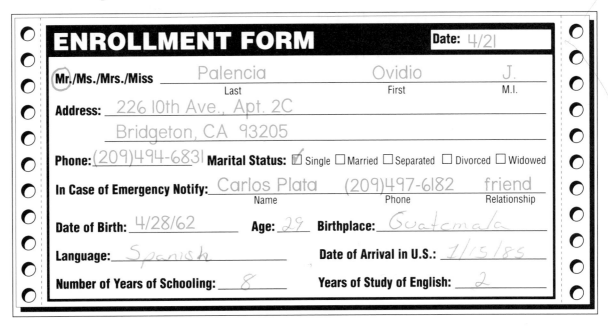

2. **Give information about Sumi.**

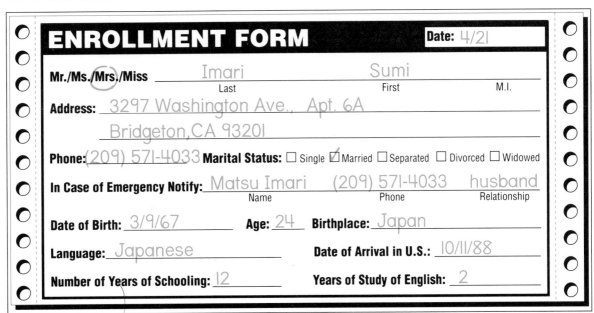

Interactions

Student B

1. **Give information about Ovidio.**

   A: When was Ovidio born?
   B: He was born on April 28, 1962.
   A: Did you say April 28, 1962?
   B: That's right.

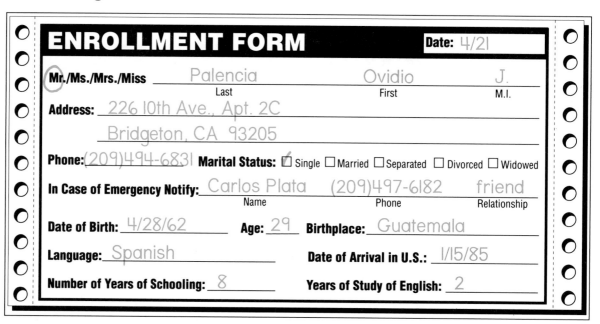

2. **Get information about Sumi. Continue the conversation. Fill in the form.**

Progress Checks ✔

1. b ☐ Fill out a form, including birthplace, date of arrival in the U.S., number of years of previous education, and number of years of study of English.

Fill out the form.

Date: _____ Phone: _____

Name: Mr./Ms./Mrs./Miss _____
                               Last   First   Middle Initial

Address: _____

_____

Age: _____ Date of Birth: _____ Place of Birth: _____

First Language: _____

Marital Status(circle): Single/Married/Widowed/Separated/Divorced

Date of Arrival in U.S. _____ Number of Years of Schooling _____

Years of English Study _____

In Case of Emergency Notify: _____
                              Name   Phone Number   Relationship

2. d ☐ Fill out a form, including names, relationships, and ages of family members.

Fill out the form.

Name	Age	Relationship to You

Progress Checks

3. a ☐ State the number of years of previous education and study of English.

c ☐ Give dates, including date of arrival in the U.S.

What are the people saying?

Do it yourself.

❖ ❖ ❖ **Memo** ❖ ❖ ❖

TO: the teacher

Have students make time lines (without names) of their lives or of imaginary characters' lives. Put the time lines in a bag and have each student take one. Students question each other (Were you born in 1956?) until they locate the author of the time line they have. Then they tell the other person's story, using the time line. (You were born in 1956.)

5 Health

Getting Started _____

1. Guess. Where are Ahmed, Betty, and Joe? What are Betty and Joe saying?

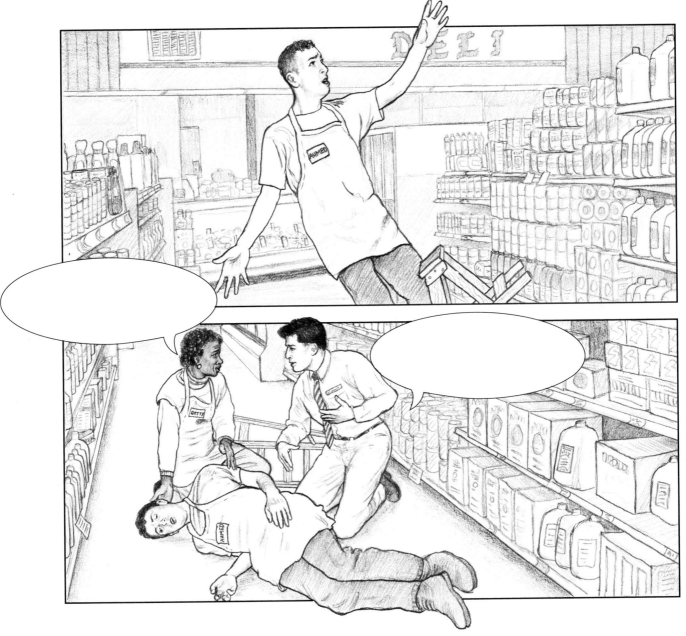

2. What can you hear?

1. **Practice.**

> Betty: Help! Joe, come here!
> Joe: What happened?
> Betty: Ahmed fell and cut his head. And I think he broke his arm.
> Joe: He needs an ambulance. You stay with Ahmed. I'm going to call 911.

2. **What can you say?**

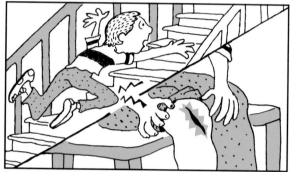

He cut his knee.

He broke his wrist.

She burned her finger.

She sprained her ankle.

3. **Talk about the injuries.**

> A: What happened?
>
> B: I think ___she sprained her toe___.

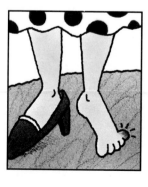   

Conversations _____

4. Practice.

Joe: The paramedics are here now.
Ahmed: What are they going to do?
Joe: They're going to take you to the emergency room.
Betty: Ahmed, I called your brother at work.
Ahmed: What did he say?
Betty: He isn't going to come here. He's going to go to the hospital. He's going to leave work in fifteen minutes.
Ahmed: OK. Thanks, Betty.
Betty: Don't worry, Ahmed. You're going to be fine.

5. Focus on grammar.

What	are they	going to	do?
Where When	are they	going to	go?

I	am (not)	going to	see the doctor	in fifteen minutes. tomorrow. next week.
They	are aren't			
She	is isn't			

6. Talk about the people.

A: What ___is he___ going to do?

B: ___He's___ going to ___stay with the boy___.

___He isn't___ going to ___call 911___.

a. stay with the boy
   call 911

b. help the boy
   leave work at 5:00

c. be fine
   stay in the hospital

Conversations _____

 7. Practice.

Ahmed:	Doctor, what can I do for this pain?
Dr. Riley:	You need some pain medicine.
	Here's a prescription.
	Take two capsules every four hours.
Ahmed:	Two capsules every four hours?
Dr. Riley:	Yes.
Ahmed:	Thanks.

8. What can you say?

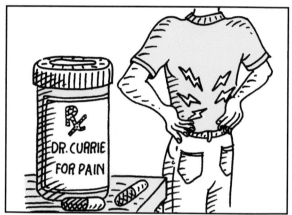

backache
capsules

cough
teaspoon

stomachache
tablespoon

fever
tablets

b
c

9. Talk about the medicine. Use the words in 8.

A: ___What can I do for this backache___?

B: You need ___pain medicine___.

Take two ___capsules___ every four hours.

Paperwork _____

d 1. **Read the labels on the medicine in Ray's medicine cabinet.**

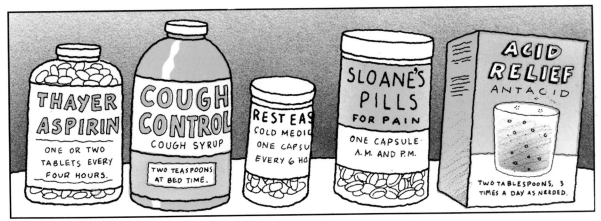

e 2. **Match.**

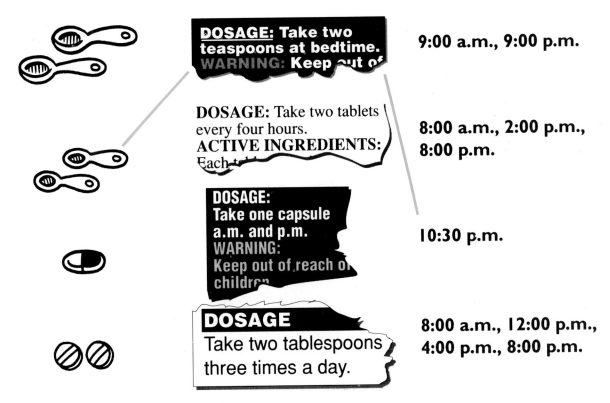

3. **Interview three classmates. Ask about the medicine they have at home. Write their answers on a separate sheet of paper.**

What do you take for a stomachache? ___Acid Relief___

What do you take for a cold? ___Rest Easy___

What do you take for a headache? ___aspirin___

Reading and Writing _____

1. What can you say about Ahmed?

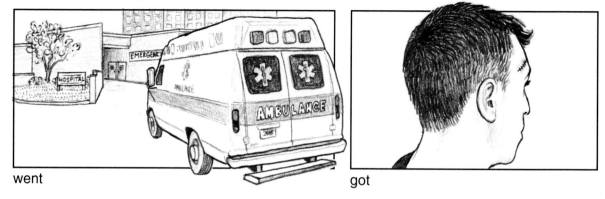

went   got

What can you say about the doctor?

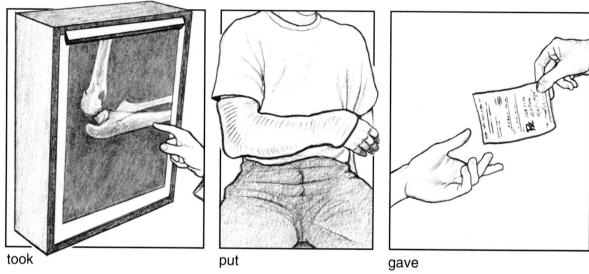

took   put   gave

2. Read about Ahmed.

    Ahmed broke his arm and cut his head. He went to the emergency room in an ambulance. He got five stitches in his head. The doctor took X-rays and put a cast on his arm. Then she gave Ahmed a prescription for pain medicine.

3. Circle *Yes, No,* or *I don't know.*

    a. Did Ahmed break his arm?   (Yes)   No   I don't know

    b. Did he go to the hospital?   Yes   No   I don't know

    c. Did his brother go to the hospital?   Yes   No   I don't know

    d. Did the doctor take X-rays?   Yes   No   I don't know

    e. Did she give Ahmed cough medicine? Yes   No   I don't know

Reading and Writing

4. Sumi got sick and went to the doctor. The doctor gave Sumi instructions. What is Sumi going to do? Use these words:

stay in bed and rest

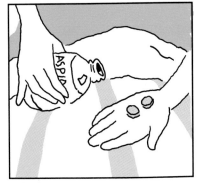

take

drink

eat

stay home

5. Read about Sumi.

   Sumi has the flu. She has a sore throat and a fever. She's going to stay in bed and rest. She's going to take two aspirin every four hours. She's going to drink a lot of liquids and eat chicken soup. She needs to call her teacher because she's going to stay home for a few days. She isn't going to go to school.

6. You are Sumi's doctor. Write instructions for Sumi. Use the words in 4.

Stay in bed and rest.

_____

_____

_____

7. A, you are Sumi's doctor. Give Sumi instructions. B, you are Sumi. Follow the instructions.

Listening Plus _____

 1. What's next?

    a. What happened?   Don't worry.   Thanks.

    b. He's going to stay in bed.   She's going to rest.   They're going to be late.

 2. Review...Write...Number.

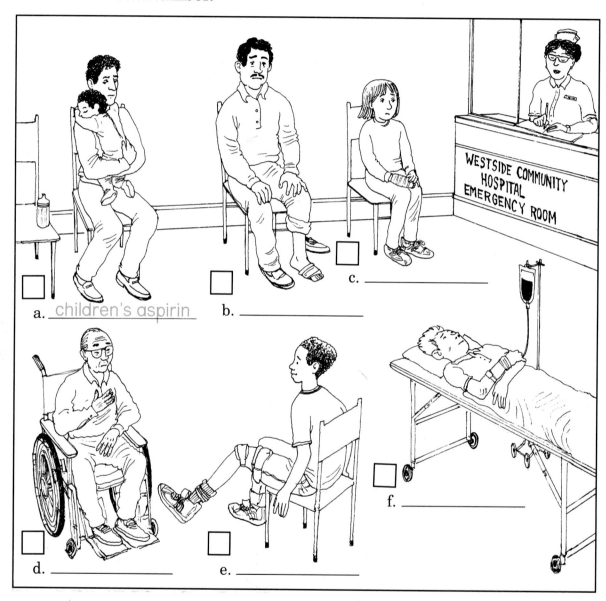

a. _children's aspirin_

b. _____

c. _____

d. _____

e. _____

f. _____

3. A, tell about a patient in 2. B, say what you heard and point.

 4. What about you?

_____

56

Interactions

Student A

g

1. **You are a patient. Get information about your cough, sore throat, fever, and sprained ankle.**

A: Doctor, what can I do for this ___cough___?

B: You need ___cough syrup___.

Take ___two teaspoons every six hours___.

A: ___Two teaspoons every six hours___?

B: That's right.

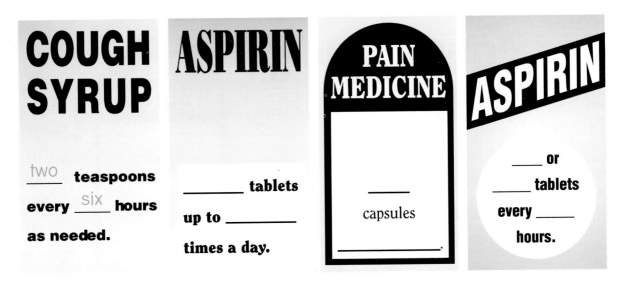

2. **You are a doctor. Give information about the medicine your patient needs.**

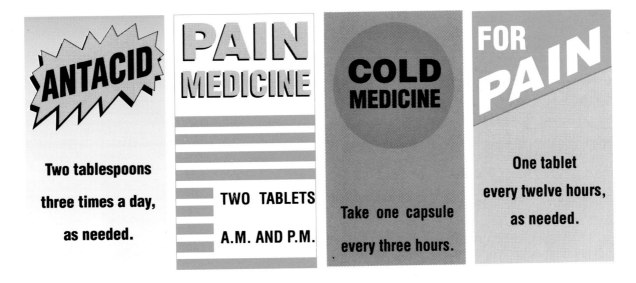

Interactions

Student B

1. **You are a doctor. Give information about the medicine your patient needs.**

    A: Doctor, what can I do for this <u>cough</u>?

    B: You need <u>cough syrup</u>.

    Take <u>two teaspoons every six hours</u>.

    A: <u>Two teaspoons every six hours</u>?

    B: That's right.

g 2. **You are a patient. Get information about your stomachache, cold, backache, and headache.**

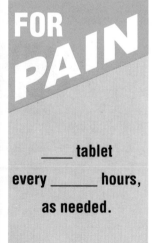

Progress Checks ✔

1. c ☐   Identify common health problems and treatment.
     d ☐   Read the names of common medicines.

Match.

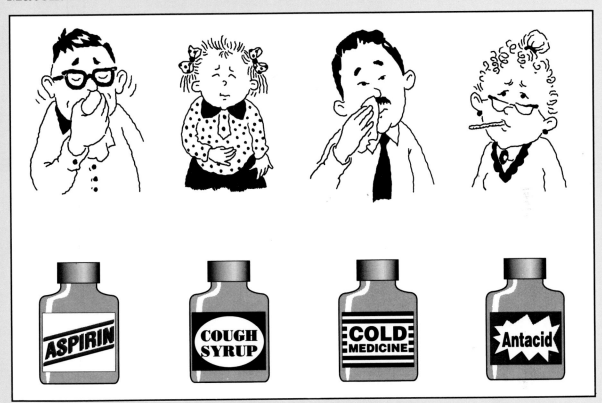

2. e ☐   Read and follow instructions on medicine labels.

Match.

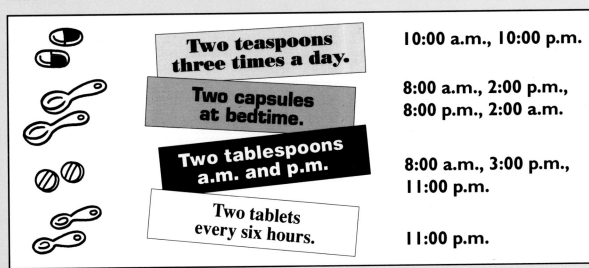

Progress Checks

3. a ☐ Identify common injuries.

What happened? Tell your partner.

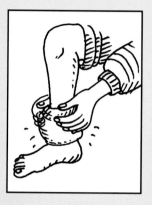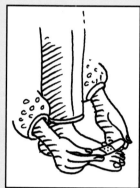

4. b ☐ Ask about medical treatment.
g ☐ Repeat instructions to check your understanding.
f ☐ Follow simple instructions for medical treatment.

What are the people saying?

Do it yourself.

❖ ❖ ❖ Memo ❖ ❖ ❖

TO: the teacher

Have students bring in empty containers of over-the-counter medicines. Put the containers in a paper bag and have each student take one. Pair students as pharmacists and customers and have the pharmacist explain the dosage to the customer.

6 Food

Getting Started

1. Guess. Where are Ramona and Mrs. Wilson? What are they saying?

2. What can you hear?

Conversations _____

1. Practice.

Ramona:	Hello, Mrs. Wilson.
Mrs. Wilson:	Hello, Ramona. Come in.
Ramona:	I'm going to the supermarket now. Do you need anything?
Mrs. Wilson:	Yes, thank you. You're very kind. Now let me see. I need some tea and some bread.
Ramona:	Do you need any potatoes?
Mrs. Wilson:	No, thanks. I don't need any potatotes, but I need some onions.

2. What can you say?

tea

bread

ice cream

potatoes

onions

apples

3. Focus on grammar.

Do you need	any	tea?
		apples?

Yes, I need	some	tea.
No, I don't need	any	apples.

4. Talk about yourself. Use the food in 2.

A: Do you need anything?

B: Yes, thank you. I need _some bread_____.

A: Do you need any ___tea_____?

B: No, thanks. I don't need any ___tea_____.

Conversations

5. Practice.

Mrs. Wilson: Please get a lot of cookies.
I really like cookies.
Ramona: How about cake?
Mrs. Wilson: No, I don't eat much cake.
Ramona: Do you want any rice?
Mrs. Wilson: Yes, get a lot of rice.
Ramona: Do you want any bananas?
Mrs. Wilson: OK. Just two. I don't eat
many bananas.

6. Focus on grammar.

| Do you eat | much | rice? |
| | many | bananas? |

| Yes, I eat | a lot of | rice. |
| | | bananas. |

| No, I don't eat | much | rice. |
| | many | bananas. |

7. Talk about the boy.

A: Does he eat ___much rice___?

B: No, he doesn't like ___rice___,

but he eats a lot of ___cookies___.

He really likes ___cookies___.

rice   apples   bread   potatoes

cookies cake bananas ice cream

Conversations

8. What can you say?

| a box | a can | a loaf | a jar | a bag | a bottle |

9. Practice.

Ramona:	Pardon me, Mrs. Wilson.
	How much bread do you want?
Mrs. Wilson:	Just one loaf, please.
Ramona:	And how many onions?
Mrs. Wilson:	Oh, three or four onions.
Ramona:	I'm sorry. How many onions?
Mrs. Wilson:	Three or four.

10. Focus on grammar.

How much	bread tea	do you want?
How many	onions potatoes	

A One	loaf. box.
One	onion.

Two	loaves. boxes. onions.

11. Talk about the food.

A: How ___much bread___ do you want?

B: ___Two loaves___, please.

A: I'm sorry. How many ___loaves___?

B: ___Two___.

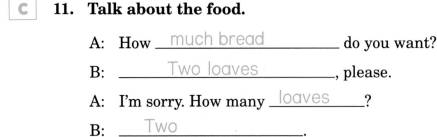

Paperwork

1. **Read the advertisement.**

$AVE FOODSMART $AVE
SPECIALS! THIS WEEK ONLY

GLOREO COOKIES! 75¢/pkg
One lb. pkg.

TUNA FISH $1.26/can
6½ oz.

APPLE JUICE $2.16/gal.

VIT D MILK 79¢/qt.

FRESH WHOLE FRYING CHICKEN 55¢/lb.

LARGE AA EGGS $1.09/doz.

d 2. **Write the abbreviations.**

a. pound _lb._   b. ounce ____   c. dozen ____

d. package ____   e. quart ____   f. gallon ____

e 3. **Interview three classmates Write their answers on a separate piece of paper.**

Where do you shop? ___Foodsmart_____

What's one food you like? ___rice_____

What's one food you don't like? ___milk_____

Reading and Writing _____

1. Donna wants to make a taco salad. What can you say about the food she needs?

2. Read about Donna.

Donna wants to make a taco salad for dinner. She's going to go to the supermarket.

She needs to buy a pound of ground beef. She also needs two medium onions, a head of lettuce, and three pounds of tomatoes. She's going to buy a pound of cheese, a can of hot peppers, and a large bag of corn chips. And she's also going to buy a quart of oil.

Donna's taco salad is going to be delicious!

3. Fill in the blanks with the amounts. Use abbreviations.

Reading and Writing _____

4. **Look at the foods. Add other foods you know. Circle the foods you like.**

onions	rice	tea	bread	eggs
apples	cookies	bananas	hot peppers	peanut butter
ice cream	tuna fish	milk	cake	ground beef
lettuce	corn chips	cheese	potatoes	tomatoes
chicken	apple juice	_____	_____	_____
_____	_____	_____	_____	_____

5. **Write a shopping list for dinner. Use the list in 3 as an example. Explain your shopping list to your partner.**

6. **Answer these questions about your shopping list. Use *some* and *any*.**

a. Are you going to buy any apples? _____

b. Are you going to buy any bread? _____

c. Are you going to buy any rice? _____

d. Are you going to buy any tea? _____

e. Are you going to buy any chicken? _____

Listening Plus _____

🎞 **1. What's next?**

    a. I'm sorry. How many?   How much?

    b. One.   One pound.

🎞 **2. Review...Write...Number.**

3. A, tell about the pictures in 2. B, say what you heard and point.

🎞 **4. What about you?**

_____

_____

Interactions

Student A

1. **Get information. Write a shopping list for B. Ask about milk, bananas, cheese, ice cream, lettuce, and tuna fish.**

   A: How ____much milk____ do you need?

   B: ____A gallon____, please.

   A: I'm sorry. How many ____gallons____?

   B: ____One____.

○	I gal. milk
○	

2. **Give information about the food you need from the supermarket.**

Interactions

Student B

1. **Give information about the food you need from the supermarket.**

   A: How __much milk__ do you need?

   B: __A gallon__, please.

   A: I'm sorry. How many __gallons__?

   B: __One__.

2. **Get information. Write a shopping list for A. Ask about peanut butter, tomatoes, eggs, bread, chicken, and apple juice.**

Progress Checks ✔

1. d ☐ Read prices, weights, measures for food, and abbreviations.

Fill in the ad. Use these prices:

79¢/qt. $1.09/doz. $1.89/jar $1.79/loaf

$1.19/can $1.49/lb. $1.59/box   89¢/head

2. e ☐ State likes and dislikes.

What is she saying?

_____ oranges.
_____ like apples.

Do it yourself.

Progress Checks ✔

3. **a** ☐   Offer to help someone.
    b ☐   Respond to offers of help.

What are the people saying?

Do it yourself.

4. **c** ☐   Ask for clarification using basic question words.

What are the people saying?

Do it yourself.

❖ ❖ ❖ Memo ❖ ❖ ❖

TO: the teacher

Bring in full-page supermarket ads and give one to each pair of
students. Assign each pair a "budget" and have them write shopping
lists that they can pay for.

7 Finding a Job

Getting Started

1. Guess. Where are Sue and Ms. Garber? What are they saying?

2. What can you hear?

Conversations

1. Practice.

Ms. Garber: May I help you?
Sue: Yes. Do you have any openings for sewing machine operators?
Ms. Garber: Yes, we do. Please fill out this application.
Sue: Thank you.

2. What can you say? Add other jobs you know.

sewing machine operator

baker

factory worker

cashier

janitor

delivery person

3. Talk about job openings. Use the conversation in 1. Use the jobs in 2.

4. Practice.

Ms. Garber: Can you come for an interview at 10:00 tomorrow?
Sue: 10:00? No. I'm sorry. I can't come then. Can I come in the afternoon?
Ms. Garber: Yes. Can you come at 1:00?
Sue: Yes, I can. Thank you.

5. Focus on grammar.

Can	they she	come in the afternoon?

Yes,	they she	can.	No,	they she	can't.

Conversations _____

b

6. Talk about appointments. Use any times.

A: Can you come for an interview at <u>1:00</u> tomorrow?

B: <u>1:00</u>? No. I'm sorry. I can't come then. Can I come in the <u>morning</u>?

A: Yes. Can you come at <u>9:30</u>?

B: Yes, I can. Thank you.

7. Practice.

Mr. Hill: Please have a seat, Mrs. Le.
Sue: Thank you.
Mr. Hill: Now, what job are you applying for?
Sue: Sewing machine operator.
Mr. Hill: Do you have any experience?
Sue: Yes, I was a sewing machine operator in Vietnam.
Mr. Hill: Do you have any experience with power machines?
Sue: No, I don't, but I can learn.

c

8. Talk about work experience. Use the jobs in 2. Use the name of your country.

A: What job are you applying for?

B: <u>Sewing machine operator</u>.

A: Do you have any experience?

B: Yes, I was a <u>sewing machine operator</u> in <u>Vietnam</u>.

   OR   No, I don't, but I can learn.

Conversations

9. Practice.

Mr. Hill: What did you do in your last job, Mrs. Le?
Sue: I was a factory worker.
Mr. Hill: Was it a full-time job?
Sue: No, it wasn't. It was part-time.
Mr. Hill: Were you happy with your job?
Sue: Yes, I was, but the factory closed.
I was laid off.

10. Focus on grammar.

Were they	happy?
	bakers?
Was he	happy
	a baker?

Yes,	they were.
	he was.

No,	they weren't.
	he wasn't.

11. Talk about the people.

A: ___Was he a cashier___ in ___El Salvador___?

B: No, ___he wasn't. He was a delivery person___.

A: ___Was he___ happy with __his__ job?

B: ___Yes, he was___.

a. cashier/El Salvador

b. office worker/Korea

c. teachers/Afghanistan

d. student/Vietnam

e. apartment
manager/Russia

f. supermarket
manager/Mexico

Grammar

2. **Carlos is speaking to a job counselor. Write the counselor's questions.**

read?   start?   use?   work?   drive?   fix?

a. _Can you use_ _____ a cash register?

b. _____ a car?

c. _____ English?

d. _____ a refrigerator?

e. _____ full-time?

f. _____ in the morning?

g. _____ a new job immediately?

3. **Look at the information about Carlos. Answer the questions in 2. Use *can* or *can't*.**

Date available _next month_
Are you available   [   ] full-time   [✓] part-time?
What shifts can you work?   [✓] 7 a.m.–3 p.m. (first)
                            [✓] 3 p.m.–11 p.m. (second)
                            [   ] 11 p.m.–7 a.m. (third)
Languages: [✓] English   [   ] Spanish   [   ] other
Do you have a driver's license?   [✓] car   [   ] bus
Can you use these machines?   [   ] sewing machine   [✓] cash register
Can you fix machines?   [✓] TV   [   ] refrigerator   [   ] stove

a. _He can use a cash register,_

but he can't use a sewing machine.

(Continued on page 142)

Grammar

1. Look at the information about Minh. Complete the interview.

	Minh Lee **102 Grove Street** **Bridgeton, CA** **93208**

Employment:

1989-1990 Part-time cashier at ABC Drugstore
Reason for leaving: laid off

Education:

1988-1991 Full-time student at Bridgeton Community College

---

was
were

A: I see you worked at the ABC Drugstore, Mr. Lee.

___Were___ _____ a delivery person?

B: __No__, __I__ __was__ a cashier.

A: _____ _____ a full-time job?

B: No, _____ _____. It _____ part-time.

I _____ a full-time student then.

A: I see. _____ _____ happy with your job at the drugstore?

B: Yes, _____ _____. I _____ very happy.

A: _____ they happy with you?

B: Yes, _____ _____.

A: Why did you leave?

B: The drugstore closed, and I _____ laid off.

(Continued on page 141)

Paperwork

1. Read Ramona's application.

EMPLOYMENT APPLICATION

NAME ___Gonzalez_____Ramona_____A._____
           Last   First   Middle Name

ADDRESS _____3496 N. 3 St_____APT. # _6B_

CITY ___Bridgeton_____STATE ___CA___ZIP CODE ___93204_____

TELEPHONE # (_209_) ___549-7286_____ SOCIAL SECURITY # _109-47-6228_

ARE YOU LEGALLY ABLE TO BE EMPLOYED IN THE U.S.? (YES) NO   U.S. CITIZEN? YES (NO)

DATE AVAILABLE ___immediately_____

ARE YOU AVAILABLE TO WORK ☑ FULL-TIME ☐ PART-TIME

CHECK SHIFTS YOU CAN WORK

☑ 7 a.m. – 3 p.m. (First)   ☐ 3 p.m. – 11 p.m. (Second)   ☐ 11 p.m. – 7 a.m. (Third)

d

2. Fill out the job application.

EMPLOYMENT APPLICATION

NAME _____
           Last   First   Middle Name

ADDRESS _____APT. # _____

CITY _____STATE _____ZIP CODE _____

TELEPHONE # (_____) _____SOCIAL SECURITY # _____

ARE YOU LEGALLY ABLE TO BE EMPLOYED IN THE U.S.? YES NO   U.S. CITIZEN? YES NO

DATE AVAILABLE _____

ARE YOU AVAILABLE TO WORK ☐ FULL-TIME ☐ PART-TIME

CHECK SHIFTS YOU CAN WORK

☐ 7 a.m. – 3 p.m. (First)   ☐ 3 p.m. – 11 p.m. (Second)   ☐ 11 p.m. – 7 a.m. (Third)

e

3. Interview three classmates. Write their information on a separate piece of paper.

Are you a U.S. citizen? ___No/Guatemala_____

When can you start? ___immediately_____

Can you work full-time? ___yes_____

What hours can you work? ___7:00 a.m.—3:00 p.m._____

Reading and Writing _____

1. **What can you say about the job notice?**

JOB NOTICE

Hospital Worker
Food Service

Full-Time

$6.00/hr.

Evening Shift
3:30 p.m. – 11:30 p.m.

2. **Read about Young Ho.**

   Young Ho is a factory worker. He works the late shift, from 12 a.m. to 8 a.m. He doesn't like the hours. He wants to work the evening shift, but there aren't any openings.

   Young Ho is going to apply for a new job. He wants to be a hospital worker. He doesn't have any experience, but he took care of his sick father in Korea. He needs to work full-time. The job pays $6.00 an hour.

   Young Ho was a teacher in Korea. In the future, he wants to be a teacher in the United States.

3. **Answer the questions on a separate piece of paper.**

   a. What does Young Ho do? ___Young Ho is a factory worker.___

   b. What shift does he want to work?

   c. What job does he want now?

   d. How much does that job pay?

   e. Does he need to work part-time or full-time?

   f. What did Young Ho do in Korea?

   g. What does Young Ho want to be in the future?

Reading and Writing _____

4. **Imagine that you need a job. Answer these questions.**

   a. What do you want to be now? ___I want to be___

   b. How much does that job pay? *$600 an hour.*

   c. Do you need to work part-time or full-time? *full Time*

5. **Write a job notice for a job you want.**
   Use your answers in 4.

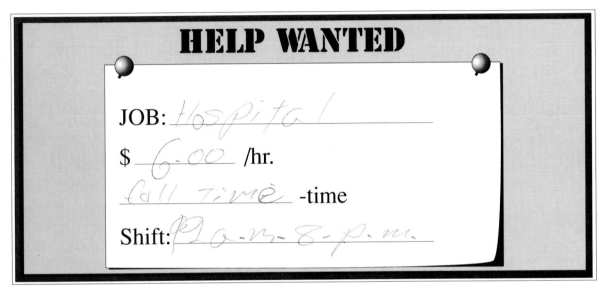

HELP WANTED

JOB: *Hospital*

$ *6.00* /hr.

full Time -time

Shift: *12 a.m. - 8 p.m.*

6. **Answer the questions.**

   a. Do you have any experience for the job in 5? *no*

   b. What did you do in your country? _____

   c. What do you want to be in the future? *full Time*

7. **Write a story about yourself. Use your answers in 4 and 6.**

   _____

   _____

   _____

   _____

   _____

8. **Read your story to your group.**

Listening Plus

1. What's next?

   a. No. I'm sorry, I can't.   Thank you.

   b. Yes, he can.   No, she can't.   Yes, she was.   No, he wasn't.

2. Review...Write...Number.

HELP WANTED ☐

**Factory Worker
Assembly
Full-Time**

$ __6.35__ /hr.

Hours: __11:30 p.m.__

__—7:30 a.m.__

a.

Employment Opportunity ☐

**Experienced
Bakers
Part-Time**

$_____ /hr.

Hours:_____

_____

b.

JOB NOTICE ☐

**Sewing Machine
Operator**

We Train!

$_____ /hr.

Hours: _____

_____

c.

**DELIVERY
PERSON** ☐

**Weekend Jobs
Top $, tips, car!**

$_____ /hr.

Hours:_____

_____

d.

Janitors ☐

**Benefits.
We train.
Raise in 4 weeks.
Full-Time only.**

$_____ /hr.

Hours: _____

_____

e.

Jobs Now! ☐

**Cashiers
6 days a week**

$_____ /hr.

Hours:_____

_____

f.

3. A, tell about the jobs in 2. B, say what you heard and point.

4. What about you?

_____

_____

Interactions _____

Student A

1. **Get information about Elena. Continue the conversation. Fill in the application.**

   A: What's Elena's phone number?
   B: It's (209) 684-9133.
   A: Can you repeat that, please?
   B: (209) 684-9133.
   A: Thanks.

EMPLOYMENT APPLICATION

NAME ___Medina_____ ___Elena_____ ___Teresa_____
              Last   First   Middle Name

ADDRESS ___6902 12th Ave._____ APT. # _8_

CITY __Bridgeton___ STATE __CA__ ZIP CODE __93205__

TELEPHONE (_209_) __684-9133__ SOCIAL SECURITY # _____

CITIZENSHIP _____ WHAT JOB ARE YOU APPLYING FOR ? _____

DATE AVAILABLE _____

ARE YOU AVAILABLE TO WORK ☐ FULL-TIME ☐ PART-TIME

CHECK SHIFTS YOU CAN WORK ☐ FIRST SHIFT ☐ SECOND SHIFT ☐ THIRD SHIFT

---

2. **Give information about Rashid.**

EMPLOYMENT APPLICATION

NAME ___Necko_____ ___Rashid_____ _____
              Last   First   Middle Name

ADDRESS ___8324 2nd Ave._____ APT. # _6A_

CITY __Bridgeton___ STATE __CA__ ZIP CODE __93201__

TELEPHONE (_209_) __338-7212__ SOCIAL SECURITY # __287-04-7912__

CITIZENSHIP __Afghanistan__ WHAT JOB ARE YOU APPLYING FOR ? __janitor__

DATE AVAILABLE __immediately__

ARE YOU AVAILABLE TO WORK ☑ FULL-TIME ☐ PART-TIME

CHECK SHIFTS YOU CAN WORK ☑ FIRST SHIFT ☑ SECOND SHIFT ☑ THIRD SHIFT

Interactions

Student B

1. Give information about Elena.

A: What's Elena's phone number?
B: It's (209) 684-9133.
A: Can you repeat that, please?
B: (209) 684-9133.
A: Thanks.

EMPLOYMENT APPLICATION

NAME ___Medina___ ___Elena___ ___Teresa___
        Last   First   Middle Name

ADDRESS ___6902 12th Ave.___ APT. # _8_

CITY ___Bridgeton___ STATE _CA_ ZIP CODE _93205_

TELEPHONE (_209_) ___684-9133___ SOCIAL SECURITY # _061-39-8814_

CITIZENSHIP ___Mexico___ WHAT JOB ARE YOU APPLYING FOR ? _cashier_

DATE AVAILABLE ___immediately___

ARE YOU AVAILABLE TO WORK ☐ FULL-TIME ☑ PART-TIME

CHECK SHIFTS YOU CAN WORK ☑ FIRST SHIFT ☐ SECOND SHIFT ☐ THIRD SHIFT

2. Get information about Rashid. Continue the conversation. Fill in the application.

EMPLOYMENT APPLICATION

NAME ___Necko___ ___Rashid___
        Last   First   Middle Name

ADDRESS ___8324 2nd Ave.___ APT. # _6A_

CITY ___Bridgeton___ STATE _CA_ ZIP CODE _93201_

TELEPHONE (_____) _____ SOCIAL SECURITY # _____

CITIZENSHIP _____ WHAT JOB ARE YOU APPLYING FOR ? _____

DATE AVAILABLE _____

ARE YOU AVAILABLE TO WORK ☐ FULL-TIME ☐ PART-TIME

CHECK SHIFTS YOU CAN WORK ☐ FIRST SHIFT ☐ SECOND SHIFT ☐ THIRD SHIFT

Progress Checks ✔

1. d ☐   Fill out a simple job application form.

Fill out the application.

APPLICATION FOR EMPLOYMENT

NAME _____
              Last   First   Middle

ADDRESS _____ APT. _____

CITY _____ STATE _____ ZIP _____

TELEPHONE (_____) _____

SOCIAL SECURITY NO. _____ CITIZENSHIP _____

JOB APPLYING FOR _____ DATE AVAILABLE_____

AVAILABLE ☐ FULL-TIME ☐ PART-TIME   FOR SHIFTS ☐ 1ST ☐ 2ND ☐ 3RD

2. a ☐   Ask about job openings.
    b ☐   Set a time for a job interview.

What are the people saying?

Do it yourself.

Progress Checks

3. c ☐ Answer questions about work experience.
e ☐ Answer questions about work shifts, hours, and starting dates.

What are the people saying?

Do it yourself.

❖ ❖ ❖ Memo ❖ ❖ ❖

TO: the teacher

Divide the students into equal numbers of job applicants, receptionists, and managers. Find out what jobs applicants want to apply for and put them in pairs to prepare for their interviews. Pair receptionists with managers and assign each pair one of the jobs chosen by the applicants. Have them decide details of the job and times for interviews. Have each receptionist make a sign to identify the job (Help Wanted: Baker). Applicants find the right office, make an appointment, and have an interview.

8 On the Job

Getting Started

1. **Guess. Where are Antonio and John? What are they saying?**

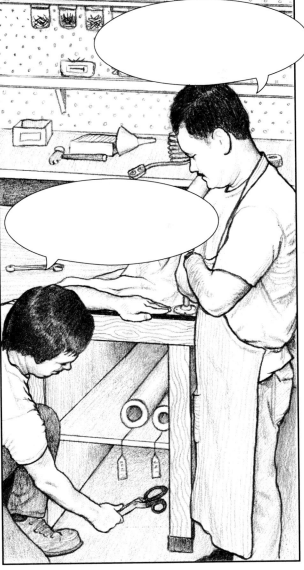

2. **What can you hear?**

Conversations _____

1. Practice.

John: Antonio, I need the scissors. Do you have them?
Antonio: The scissors? I saw them a minute ago.
John: Never mind. I found them. They were under the table.
Antonio: Can I have the screwdriver?
John: Hmm. It's not on the pegboard. Maybe Bill took it. Ask him.

2. What can you say?

hammer

scissors

screwdriver

pliers

wrench

tape measure

nails

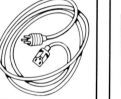
extension cord

screws

saw

3. Focus on grammar.

John saw	me.
	you.
	us.
	them.
	him.
	her.
	it.

Ask	Bill.
	him.
	Betty.
	her.

Bill took	the screwdriver.
	it.
	the scissors.
	them.

4. Talk about the tools in 2.

A: I need ____the hammer____. Do you have ____it____?

B: Maybe ____Ray and Van____ took ____it____.

   Ask ____them____.

a. Ray and Van   b. Sue   c. Bill   d. Joe and Betty

Conversations

5. Practice.

Mr. Ross: Antonio, where were you yesterday?
Antonio: My son was sick. I took him to the doctor.
Mr. Ross: OK, but call me next time.
Antonio: I'm really sorry. I was worried and I forgot.
Mr. Ross: How is your son now?
Antonio: He's going to be fine, thanks.

6. Focus on grammar.

Where	were	they	last night?
	was	he	this morning?

They	were	at	home.
He	was		work.
			school.

7. What can you say?

I was sick.

My babysitter didn't come.

My car broke down.

b **8. Talk about lateness or absence. Use the excuses in 7.**

A: Where were you _____ yesterday _____?

B: _____ I was sick _____.

A: OK, but call me next time.

Conversations

9. Practice.

Antonio: Can you cash this check, please?
Teller: Do you have any identification?
Antonio: Yes. Here's my driver's license.
Teller: Thank you. Oh, you need to endorse your check.
Antonio: Sorry. I forgot.
Teller: No problem.

10. What can you say?

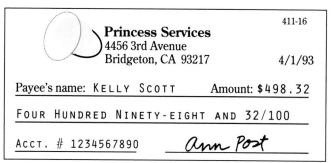

check

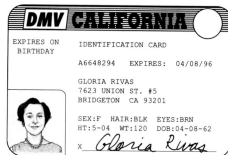

ID card

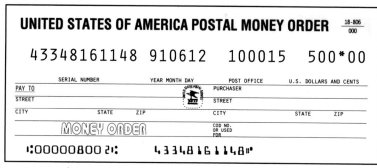

money order

driver's license

11. Talk about getting cash. Use the conversation in 9 and the words in 10. A, sign your name.

ENDORSE HERE

DO NOT WRITE STAMP OR SIGN BELOW THIS LINE
RESERVED FOR FINANCIAL INSTITUTION USE

MAXIMUM VALUE
SEVEN HUNDRED DOLLARS

ENDORSEMENT SIGNATURE

Paperwork

1. Antonio works 40 hours a week. He makes $5.75 an hour. He gets paid every week. He cashes his check at Bridgeton National Bank. Read Antonio's paycheck.

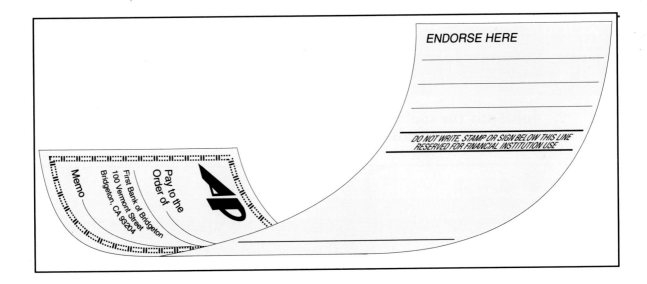

AMERICAN PRODUCTS, INC.
7801 JEFFERSON STREET
BRIDGETON, CA 93207

1795

November 8 19 *91*

Pay to the Order of _*Antonio Medina*_ $ *208.70*

Two Hundred Eight and 70/100 _____ Dollars

First Bank of Bridgeton
100 Vermont Street
Bridgeton, CA 93204

B. Franklin Pierce

Memo _____

⑆012000089⑆ 099 345678L2⑆ 1795

ENDORSE HERE
_____
_____
_____

DO NOT WRITE, STAMP OR SIGN BELOW THIS LINE
RESERVED FOR FINANCIAL INSTITUTION USE

Pay to the Order of

First Bank of Bridgeton
100 Vermont Street
Bridgeton, CA 93204

Memo

2. How much does Antonio make every week? _____

   What's his take-home pay? _____

3. Interview three classmates. Write their information on a separate piece of paper.

   Do you have a job? _____ yes _____

   Where do you cash checks? _____ Bridgeton National Bank _____

   What ID do you have? _____ driver's license _____

Reading and Writing _____

1. **What can you say about the tools on this worktable? Use these words:**

on the top shelf   on the pegboard   to the right of the saw
on the middle shelf   on the worktable   to the left of the pliers
on the bottom shelf   to the left of the shelves

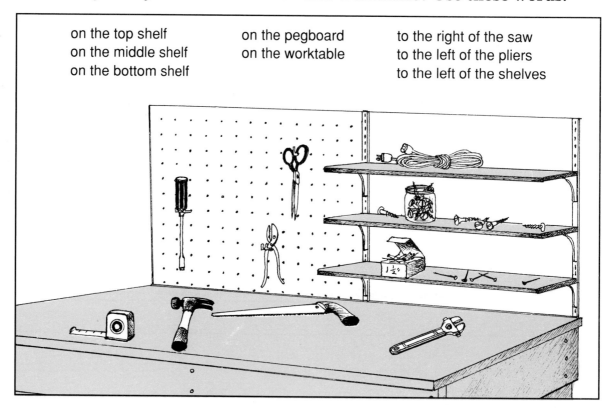

2. **John put the tools away in the storeroom. He didn't read the list on the storeroom wall. Read the list.**

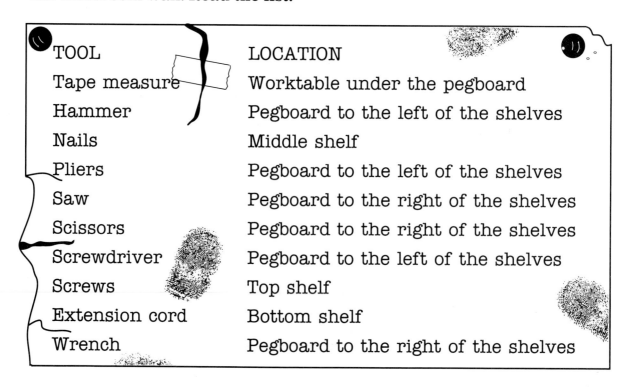

TOOL	LOCATION
Tape measure	Worktable under the pegboard
Hammer	Pegboard to the left of the shelves
Nails	Middle shelf
Pliers	Pegboard to the left of the shelves
Saw	Pegboard to the right of the shelves
Scissors	Pegboard to the right of the shelves
Screwdriver	Pegboard to the left of the shelves
Screws	Top shelf
Extension cord	Bottom shelf
Wrench	Pegboard to the right of the shelves

90

3. **What tools did John put in the wrong place? Circle them.**

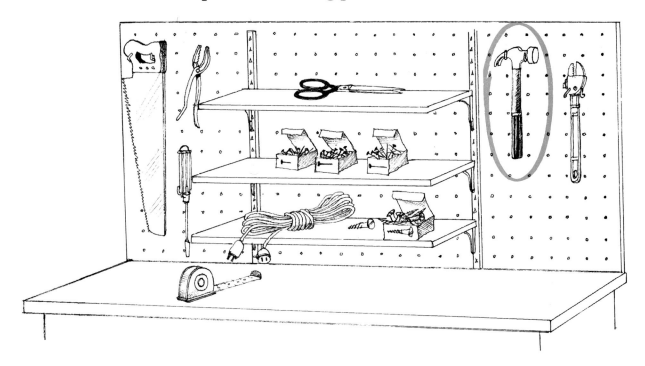

4. **Imagine that you are Mr. Ross. Write a note to John. Tell him where to put the tools.**

> John, you put some tools in the wrong place. Put the hammer on the pegboard to the left of the shelves.
>
>   Thanks,
>   Jim Ross

5. **Show your note to your partner.**

Listening Plus

1. What's next?

a. Sorry. I forgot. Never mind. I found it. No problem.

b. Bill took them. Bill took it. Bill took her.

2. Review...Write...Number.

hammer

3. A, give the location of something in 2. B, say what you heard and point.

4. What about you?

_____

_____

Interactions

Student A

1. **Give information. Tell B where to put the boxes in the storeroom. B's picture has the window and the shelves.**

   A: Put the ___books on the bottom shelf,___
      ___to the right of the window___.

   B: Where?

   A: ___To the right of the window___.

   B: OK.

2. **Get information. Draw boxes in the storeroom and label them.**

Interactions

Student B

g   **1. Get information. Draw boxes in the storeroom and label them.**

A: Put the ___books on the bottom shelf,___
   ___to the right of the window___.

B: Where?

A: ___To the right of the window___.

B: OK.

2. **Give information. Tell A where to put the boxes in the storeroom. A's picture has the shelves.**

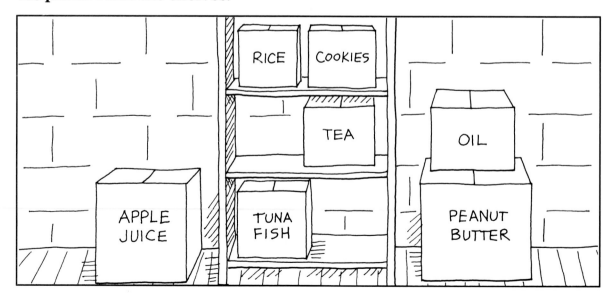

Progress Checks

1. f ☐ Endorse a check or money order.

Endorse this check.

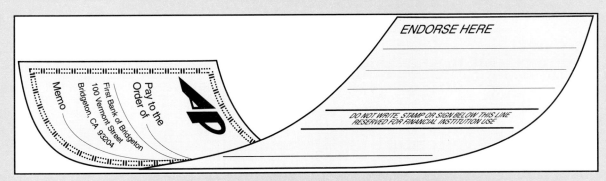

2. c ☐ Ask to cash a check or money order.

d ☐ Show proper I D.

What are the people saying?

Do it yourself.

3. b ☐ Give simple excuses for lateness or absence.

What are the people saying?

Do it yourself.

Progress Checks ✔

4. a ☐ State a need for tools.
    e ☐ Apologize for forgetting something.

What are the people saying?

Do it yourself.

5. g ☐ Follow spoken instructions about where to put things.

What are they doing?

Do it yourself.

❖ ❖ ❖ Memo ❖ ❖ ❖

TO: the teacher
Have students work in pairs to prepare excuses. Then, in new pairs, "employees" phone "supervisors" to say that they are going to be late or that they can't come to work today. Encourage students to expand the conversations as much as they can.

---

9 Clothing

Getting Started

1. **Guess. Where are Gloria, her daughters, and the sales clerk? What are Gloria and the sales clerk saying?**

2. **What can you hear?**

Conversations _____

  1. Practice.

Gloria: Excuse me. Do you work here?
Clerk: Yes, I do. May I help you?
Gloria: Yes, please. Where are the children's jeans?
Clerk: For girls or boys?
Gloria: Girls.
Clerk: Over there next to the jackets.
Gloria: Thanks. And do you have these shoes in size 8?
Clerk: Let me check.

2. What can you say?

| shirt | jeans | blouse | pants | shoes |

| socks | sweater | skirt | dress | jacket |

3. Talk about the clothes in 2.

A: May I help you?

B: Yes, please. Where are the ___shirts___?

A: Over there, next to the ___sweaters___.

B: Thanks. And do you have ___this jacket___ in ___large___?

A: Let me check.

Conversations _____

4. What can you say?

big   small   long   short

y

5. Practice.

Lucy: Mommy, how does this blouse look?
Gloria: It looks too big. Try the other blouse on.
        It's smaller than the yellow blouse.
Lucy: OK, Mommy. This blouse fits.
Gloria: Good. Now try the white jeans on.
Lucy: They're too long.
Gloria: OK. Try the black jeans on.
        They're shorter than the white jeans.
Lucy: Oh, good. These jeans fit, Mommy.

6. Focus on grammar.

big	bigger
small	smaller
long	longer
short	shorter

The white	shirt	is	smaller than the yellow	shirt.
	shirts	are		shirts.

7. Talk about the clothes.

A: How ____does this sweater____ look?

B: ____It looks____ too ____small____.

   Try ____the other sweater____ on.

   ____It's bigger____ than the ____yellow sweater____.

y

z

Unit 9

99

Conversations

8. What can you say?

cash

charge

receipt

9. Practice.

Cashier: Is that cash or charge?
Gloria: Cash.
Cashier: That comes to $27.30.
Gloria: Here you are.
Cashier: Here's your change, $2.70.
And here's your receipt.
Gloria: Excuse me. I gave you $40.00.
My change should be $12.70.
Cashier: I'm sorry. Here you are.
Gloria: That's OK. No problem.

10. Talk about a purchase. B, figure out the change.

A: Is that cash or charge?

B: Cash.

A: That comes to _____$5.80_____.

B: Here you are.

A: Here's your change. And here's your receipt.

B: Excuse me. I gave you $20.00.

The total is _____$5.80_____.

My change should be _____$14.20_____.

A: I'm sorry. Here you are.

B: That's OK. No problem.

a. $5.80   b. $8.00   c. $2.25   d. $9.50

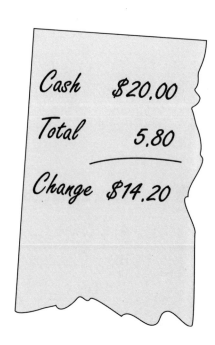

Cash $20.00
Total   5.80
_____
Change $14.20

1. **Sue and Van Lee went shopping at J Mart with their son Tran and their daughter Minh. Read Sue's list.**

	Sue	Van	Tran	Minh
pants	10	30/32	14	8
shirt	10	S	16	8
dress	10	—	—	8
jacket	M	S	L	S

2. **These are the Lee family's new clothes. Write their names next to their clothes.**

Minh

3. **Interview three classmates. Use a separate piece of paper.**

Where do you shop for clothes? _____ J Mart _____

Do you shop for women's, men's, or children's clothes? _____ women's, men's, children's _____

Do you charge or pay cash? _____ pay cash _____

Reading and Writing _____

1. **Gloria couldn't find her daughter, Bonita. What can you say about Bonita? Use these words.**

tall   short   fat   thin   young   old

2. **Gloria gave a description of Bonita to the store manager. Read Gloria's description of Bonita.**

   My daughter's name is Bonita Rivas. She's four years old. She's tall and thin. She's 3 feet 4 inches tall, and she weighs 34 pounds. She has long black hair and brown eyes. She's wearing a white shirt, black pants, white socks, and sneakers.

3. **Fill in the missing person form for Bonita.**

MISSING PERSON FORM

Name: Bonita Rivas   **Age:** ____ yrs.

Height: ____ ' ____ "   **Weight:** ____ lbs.

Hair color: _____   **Eye color:** _____

Clothing: _____

They found Bonita.

Reading and Writing

4. What can you say?

| striped | polka-dotted | print | plaid | checked |

5. Imagine that one of the people in 4 is missing. Fill in the missing person form.

═══════════ **Missing Person** ═══════════

Name:_____ Age: _____ yrs.

Height: _____ft. _____in. Weight: _____ lbs.

Hair color: _____Eye color:_____

Clothing: _____

_____

_____

_____

6. Write a description of the person. Use a separate piece of paper.

7. Read your description to your group. Group, point to the person in 4.

Listening Plus _____

1. What's next?

    a. Let me check.   That's OK.   I'm sorry.

    b. It looks too big.   They look too small.

2. Review...Write...Number.

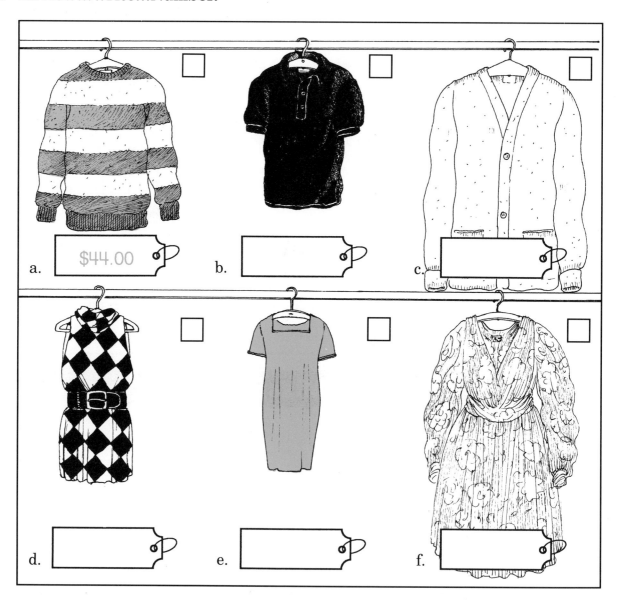

a. $44.00

b.

c.

d.

e.

f.

3. A, describe the clothes in 2. B, say what you heard and point.

4. What about you?

_____

_____

Interactions

Student A

1. **Get information. Fill in the prices.**

   A: Excuse me. Do you have

      ___black pants___ in ___size 32/36___ ?

   B: No. I'm sorry. We don't.

   A: Thank you.

   A: Excuse me. Do you have

      ___grey pants___ in ___size 32/32___ ?

   B: Yes, we do.

   A: How much ___are they___ ?

   B: ___$20.00___ .

   Shopping List

   black pants, size 32/36 ___no___

   gray pants, size 32/32 ___$20.00___

   white sweater, size S _____

   yellow sweater, size M _____

   socks, size L _____

   black shoes, size 10 _____

   black shoes, size 11 _____

   Total _____

f 2. **Give information about the clothes.**

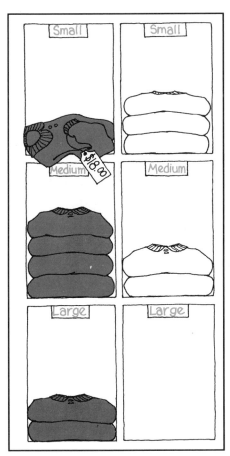

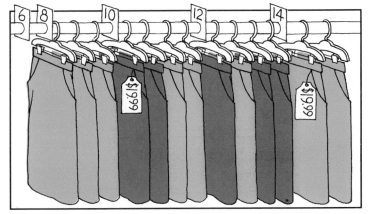

Interactions

Student B

f

1. **Give information about the clothes.**

A: Excuse me. Do you have

___black pants___ in ___size 32/36___?

B: No. I'm sorry. We don't.

A: Thank you.

A: Excuse me. Do you have

___grey pants___ in ___size 32/32___?

B: Yes, we do.

A: How much ___are they___?

B: ___$20.00___.

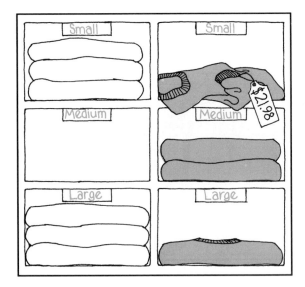

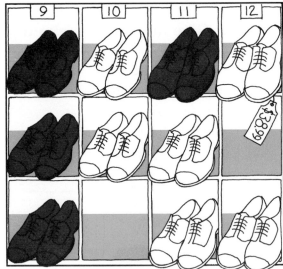

2. **Get information. Fill in the prices.**

Shopping List

yellow skirt, size 12 _____   plaid jacket, size 12 _____

gray skirt, size 14 _____   white sweater, size M _____

gray blouse, size 10 _____   Total _____

white blouse, size 12 _____

Progress Checks

1. **f** ☐   Read sizes and prices.

Fill in the prices.

a. Large jacket _____

b. Medium sweater _____

c. Small shirt _____

2. **a** ☐   Name common articles of clothing.
   b ☐   Ask for the size you need.

What are the people saying?

Do ___ sweater ___ small?

Let me check.

Do it yourself.

Progress Checks

3. e ☐ Give simple descriptions of people.

What are the people saying?

> He isn't tall and he isn't short.
> _____ hair and brown eyes.
> _____ a jacket.

> It's Boris!

Do it yourself.

4. c ☐ Respond to questions about payment.
   d ☐ Identify incorrect change and ask for the right amount.

What are the people saying?

> _____ $22.00.
> _____?

> Cash.

> Here's _____.

> Excuse me. _____ $40.00.
> _____ $18.00.

> _____
> Here you are.

Do it yourself.

❖ ❖ ❖ Memo ❖ ❖ ❖

TO: the teacher
Create a classroom clothing store with departments, aisles, fitting rooms and check-out counters. Use play money and pictures of clothing with sizes and prices marked. Students become shoppers, sales people, and cashiers.

10 Transportation

Getting Started _____

1. **Guess. Where are Donna and Young Ho? What are they saying?**

2. **What can you hear?**

Conversations _____

1. Practice.

Donna: What are you going to do this weekend, Young Ho?
Young Ho: I'm going to see my grandparents in Los Angeles.
Donna: That's nice. Do they ever come to Bridgeton?
Young Ho: No, never. They hardly ever travel.
Donna: How do you get there?
Young Ho: I usually take the train, but this weekend I'm going to take the bus.
Donna: How long is the trip?
Young Ho: It takes about three hours by train. It's usually four hours by bus.

2. Focus on grammar.

| Do you ever | take the train? |
| | go to Los Angeles? |

Yes,	always.
	usually.
	sometimes.

| The trip | usually takes | four hours. |
| | is   usually | |

| No, | hardly ever. |
| | never. |

3. What can you say?

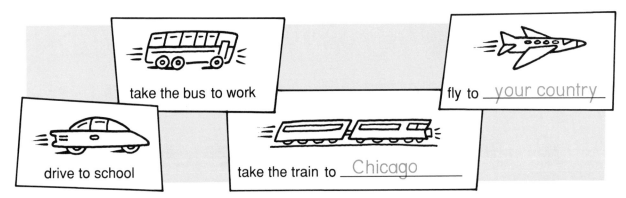

take the bus to work

fly to _your country_

drive to school

take the train to _Chicago_

4. Talk about yourself. Use the words in 3.

A: Do you ever _drive_ to _school_?   OR   A: Do you ever _drive_

B: Yes, _sometimes_.   to _school_?

A: How long is the trip?   B: No, _never_.

B: It's usually about _30 minutes_.

110   Unit 10

Conversations

5. Practice.

Young Ho: What time does the Los Angeles bus leave, please?
Agent: It leaves at 9:45.
Young Ho: And what time does it get there?
Agent: 1:37 p.m.
Young Ho: Is there a later bus?
Agent: Yes, there's a 12:45 bus. It gets to Los Angeles at 4:50 p.m.
Young Ho: Thanks a lot.

6. What can you say?

7. Talk about the bus schedules.

A: What time does the ____Denver____ bus leave, please?

B: ___5:08 a.m.___

A: And what time does it get there?

B: ___11:55 p.m.___

A: Thank you.

BUS SCHEDULE	To: Denver		To: Las Vegas		To: San Diego	
	Departs:	5:08 a.m.	Departs:	5:13 p.m.	Departs:	3:09 p.m.
	Arrives:	11:55 p.m.	Arrives:	10:50 p.m.	Arrives:	5:39 p.m.

BUS SCHEDULE	To: Chicago		To: Washington, D.C.		To: Miami	
	Departs:	7:45 a.m.	Departs:	7:12 a.m.	Departs:	12:15 p.m.
	Arrives:	9:15 p.m.	Arrives:	6:41 p.m.	Arrives:	11:06 p.m.

Conversations _____

8. What can you say?

one-way

round-trip

9. Practice.

Young Ho: I'd like a ticket to Los Angeles, please.
Agent: One-way or round-trip?
Young Ho: Round-trip. How much is it?
Agent: $42.00.
Young Ho: Here you are.
Agent: And here's your ticket, round-trip to L.A. Have a nice trip.
Young Ho: Thanks.

10. Talk about one-way and round-trip tickets.

A: I'd like a ticket to _New York_, please.

B: One-way or round trip?

A: _One-way_. How much is it?

B: _$25.00_.

A: OK. Here you are.

B: And here's your ticket, _one-way_ to _New York_.

Have a nice trip.

A: Thanks.

New York		Miami		Chicago	
One-Way	Round-Trip	One-Way	Round-Trip	One-Way	Round-Trip
$25.00	$42.00	$34.00	$68.00	$87.50	$175.00

Paperwork _____

1. Sumi sees these signs on her way to school. Read the signs.

d

2. Write the number of the sign in 1.

a. Disabled Parking Only   _2_

b. Don't Walk   ____

c. School Crossing   ____

d. Railroad Crossing   ____

e. Pedestrian Crossing   ____

f. Walk   ____

3. Interview three classmates. Use the numbers from 1. Write their answers on a separate piece of paper.

Which signs are the same in your country? _____0_____

Which signs are the same in the place where you live now? ____3,5____

Which signs can you see on your way to school? ____1,2,3,4,5,6____

Reading and Writing _____

1. What can you say about Pablo's trip to the United States?

2. Read Pablo's story about his first trip to the United States.

    I'm from a little village in Mexico. In 1960, I wanted to come to the United States. I waited a year for my visa. I left home on September 2, 1961.

    First, my father drove me to the bus station in his truck and I bought a ticket to Mexico City. I was on the bus for two days. My uncle met me at the bus station in Mexico City. He took me to the airport there.

    I flew to Los Angeles, California. I arrived in the United States on September 5, 1961. My brother Carlos met me at the airport. He took me to his house. I felt very tired, but very happy.

3. Circle the answer that completes the sentence correctly.

a. Pablo is from ____.	a village	Los Angeles	Mexico City
b. He left home on ____.	2/9/61	6/2/61	9/2/61
c. He went to Mexico City ____.	by car	by bus	by plane
d. Pablo's uncle took him to ____.	Mexico City	the airport	the bus station
e. Pablo went to Los Angeles ____.	by bus	by train	by plane
f. Carlos took Pablo to ____.	his house	Los Angeles	the airport

Reading and Writing _____

4. **Draw lines. Show your trip from your country to the United States. Use Pablo's trip as an example.**

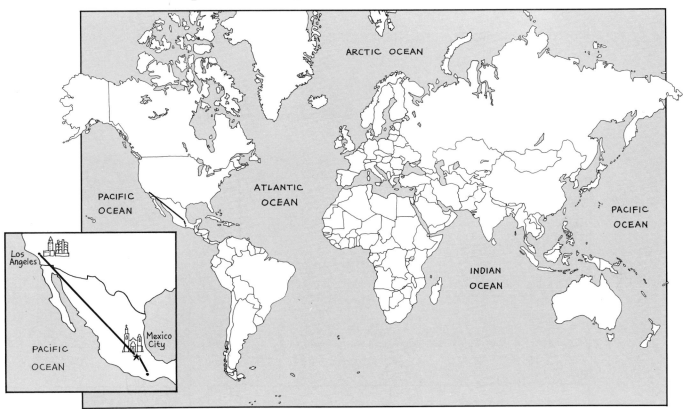

e 5. **Answer these questions about yourself. Use a separate piece of paper.**

    a. Where are you from? ___ I'm from _____.

    b. When did you leave home?

    c. When did you get to the United States?

    d. Who came with you?

    e. How did you get here?

    f. Who met you?

    g. Where did you go?

    h. How did you feel?

6. **Write a story about yourself. Use Pablo's story as an example. Use a separate piece of paper.**

7. **Read your story to your group.**

Listening Plus _____

1. What's next?

    a.   Tired but happy.   That's nice.   Have a nice trip.

    b.   About an hour.   7:15.   October 17, 1989.

2. Review...Write...Number.

a.
```
bus
N.Y. City
leaves  7:30 a.m
arrives  9:55 p.m
```

b.
```
plane
N.Y. City
dep. ____
arr. ____
```

c.
```
train
Los Angeles
lv. ____
arr. ____
```

d.
```
bus
St. Louis
lvs. ____
arrives ____
```

e.
```
plane
Denver
dep. ____
arr. ____
```

f.
```
train
Denver
departs ____
arrives ____
```

3. A, tell where you want to go and how you want to travel. B, say what you heard and point.

4. What about you?

_____

_____

Interactions _____

Student A

1. **Give information about Van's trip to the United States.**
   Continue the conversation.

   A: Van is from Vietnam.
      He left Vietnam on September 14, 1990.
   B: How do you spell Vietnam?
   A: V-I-E-T-N-A-M.
   B: Thanks. Can you repeat the date?
   A: September 14, 1990.

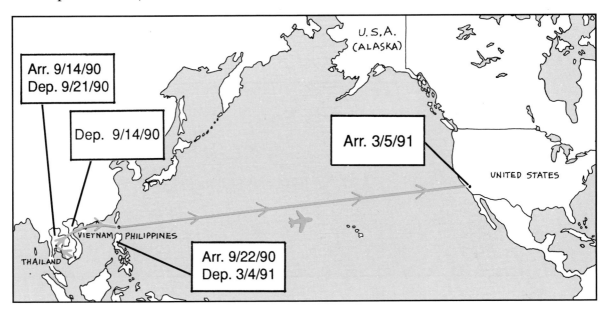

2. **Get information about Olga's trip to the United States.**

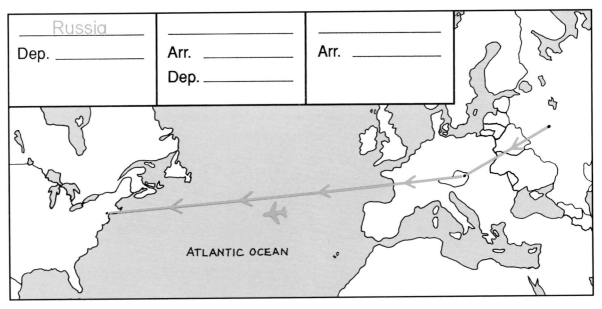

Interactions

Student B

1. **Get information about Van's trip to the United States.**

   A: Van is from Vietnam.
   He left Vietnam on September 14, 1990.
   B: How do you spell Vietnam?
   A: V-I-E-T-N-A-M.
   B: Thanks. Can you repeat the date?
   A: September 14, 1990.

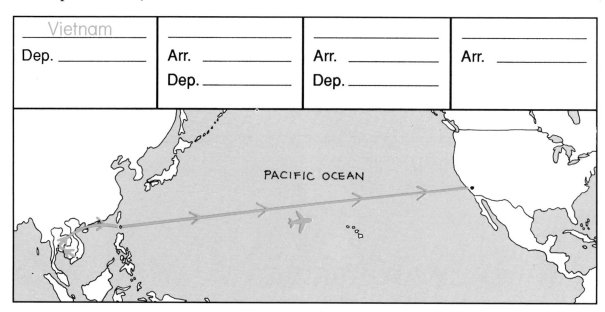

Vietnam			
Dep. _____	Arr. _____ Dep. _____	Arr. _____ Dep. _____	Arr. _____

2. **Give information about Olga's trip to the United States. Continue the conversation.**

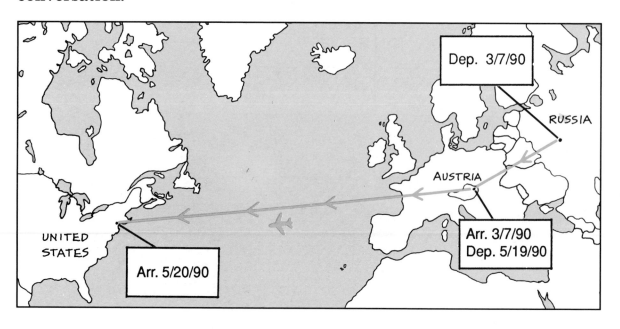

Progress Checks ✔

1. d ☐ Read common traffic and pedestrian signs.

Match.

Disabled Parking Only

Walk

Don't Walk

Railroad Crossing

School Crossing

Pedestrian Crossing

2. a ☐ Ask and answer questions about departure and arrival times.
   b ☐ Read departure and arrival schedules.

What are the people saying?

TO	DEPARTS	ARRIVES
DENVER	11:00 A.M.	1:00 P.M.

Do it yourself.

TO	DEPARTS	ARRIVES
LOS ANGELES	11:00 A.M.	12:00 P.M.
CHICAGO	1:30 P.M.	4:30 P.M.
NEW YORK	2:05 P.M.	4:38 P.M.
MIAMI	2:45 P.M.	4:15 P.M.

Progress Checks

3. c ☐ Buy travel tickets, asking about fares.

What are the people saying?

Do it yourself.

4. e ☐ Give information about the trip from your home country to the United States.

What are the people saying?

Do it yourself.

❖ ❖ ❖ **Memo** ❖ ❖ ❖

TO: the teacher

In pairs, "ticket agents" name their airline; decide destinations, ticket prices, and schedules; and set up their ticket counter. Also in pairs, "tourists" decide where to go, when to leave, and how much they can pay. Tourists find the airline that best meets their needs.

Grammar Summaries

Present Tense of *be* (review)

I'm	(not)	from Mexico.
We're		
You're		
They're		
He's		
She's		
It's		

Am	I	late?
Are	we	
	you	
	they	
Is	he	
	she	
	it	

Yes,	I	am.	No,	I'm	not.
	we	are.		we're	
	you			you're	
	they			they're	
	he	is.		he's	
	she			she's	
	it			it's	

What color	are they?
Who	is it?
How old	

Simple Present Tense (review)

I	need	a deposit.
We		
You		
They		
He	needs	
She		
It		

I	don't	need a deposit.
We		
You		
They		
He	doesn't	
She		
It		

Do	I	need a deposit?
	we	
	you	
	they	
Does	he	
	she	
	it	

Yes,	I do.	No,	I don't.
	he does.		he doesn't.

How	do you	go?
What time	does he	

Past Tense of *be*

I / He / She / It	was / wasn't	late.
You / We / They	were / weren't	

Was	I / he / she / it	late?
Were	we / you / they	

Yes,	he was.
	they were.

No,	he wasn't.
	they weren't.

Simple Past Tense

I / You / We / They / He / She / It		passed / took	the test.
	didn't	pass / take	

Did	I / you / we / they / he / she / it	pass / take	the test?

Yes,	I / he	did.

No,	I / he	didn't.

Where / When / How long	did you study English?

Future Time with *be going to*

I'm / You're / We're / They're / He's / She's / It's	going to leave.

I'm	not	going to leave.
You aren't		
He isn't		

Am I	going to be late?
Are you	
Is he	

Yes,	I am.
	we are.
	he is.

No,	I'm not.
	we aren't.
	he isn't.

Where	are you	going to go?
When	is he	

Imperatives (review)

(Don't)	Go	to work.
	Take	two aspirin.
	Stay	in bed.

There is / There are

There's	a bus	to Chicago.
There are	trains	

Is there a bus	to Chicago?
Are there trains	

Yes, there	is.
	are.

No, there	isn't.
	aren't.

122

Need to, Want to, Have to

I	want to	get an ID card.
	need to	
	have to	

Can

I	can	come in the afternoon.
	can't	

Can	you	come in the afternoon?
	she	

Yes,	I	can.	No,	I	can't.
	you			you	
	she			she	

What shifts	can you work?
When	

Object Pronouns

John saw	me.
	you.
	us.
	them.
	him.
	her.
	it.

Some, Any, Much, Many, A lot of

I	need	some	tea.
		a lot of	bananas.
	don't need	any	tea.
		much	
		any	bananas.
		many	

Do you need	any	tea?
		bananas?
	much	tea?
	many	bananas?

How much tea	do you need?
How many bananas	

Adjectives with *-er*

They're	bigger	than the white jeans.
	smaller	
	longer	
	shorter	

Adverbs of frequency

The trip	always takes	four hours.
	is always	

Do you ever	take the train?
	drive?

Yes,	always.	No,	hardly ever.
	usually.		never.
	sometimes.		

Location

It's	across	the street.
	across from	the school.
	around	the corner.
	down	the block.
	on	the next block.
		two blocks away.
	to the left of	the table.
	to the right of	
	under	

Tapescript

Exercise 1. What's next?

a.

1. A: Earl, could you come over here a minute, please? I want you to meet my sister Rachel. Rachel, this is Earl.
What's next?

2. A: Does your teacher speak Spanish?
   B: Yes. He speaks English, Spanish, and a little Chinese.
What's next?

3. A: Bye, Ellen. Bye, Marjorie. Good night, Antonio. See you next week.
What's next?

4. A: Tracy, this is Max Spiegel.
   B: Hello, Max. I'm Tracy Simon.
What's next?

5. A: Well, it's late. Time to go home.
   B: Yeah. Me too. See you tomorrow.
   A: OK. Good night.
What's next?

6. A: So how do you like your English class?
   B: I like it a lot. The teacher is good and there are two students from my country.
What's next?

b.

1. A: Have you met the new guy — Ovidio?
   B: I met him yesterday. He seems very nice. Is he from Mexico?
What's next?

2. A: Hi, Conchita. Where are Nola and Ricky? Are they coming to class tonight?
What's next?

3. A: Look, Vladimir. Do you see that man over there? Is he our new teacher?
What's next?

4. A: Where are you from, Tranh? Are you from Vietnam?
What's next?

5. A: Hi, Le. How are you doing?
   B: Fine, Katya. Nice to see you. Where are your brothers? Are they here tonight?
What's next?

6. A: Excuse me. Are you from El Salvador?
   B: Uh-huh.
   A: Is your last name Diaz?
   B: Yes, it is.
   A: Are you Maria Diaz's brother?
What's next?

**Exercise 2. Review... Write... Number.
Write the countries and languages.**

a. A: Are you from the United States?
   B: No. I'm from Canada, originally.
   A: Is that with a C?
   B: Yes, C-A-N-A-D-A.
   A: C-A-N-A-D-A. And what's your first language?
   B: English.
   A: I'm sorry. Did you say English?
   B: Yes. E-N-G-L-I-S-H.
   A: E-N-G... ?

B: L-I-S-H. English.

b. A: What country are you from, Victor?
   B: Russia.
   A: How do you spell that?
   B: R-U-S-S-I-A.
   A: R-U-S-S-I-A?
   B: Yes.
   A: OK. And what's your first language?
   B: Russian.
   A: Excuse me?
   B: Russian. R-U-S-S-I-A-N.
   A: R-U-S-S-I-A-N. Got it.

c. A: And where are you from originally?
   B: I'm from Egypt.
   A: Would you mind spelling that for me, please?
   B: Egypt. E-G-Y-P-T.
   A: I'm sorry. Could you spell it more slowly please?
   B: Sure. E-G-Y-P-T.
   A: And what language do you speak?
   B: I speak Arabic. A-R-A-B-I-C.
   A: A-R-A-B-I-C. Thanks.

d. A: Where are you from?
   B: I'm from India.
   A: How do you spell that?
   B: I-N-D-I-A.
   A: I-N... what?
   B: I-N-D-I-A.
   A: And do you speak Indian?
   B: No. I speak Hindi.
   A: Could you repeat that?
   B: Hindi. H-I-N-D-I.
   A: H-I-N-D-I. Thanks.

e. A: What's your country of origin, Mei Lee?
   B: Excuse me?
   A: Uh, where are you from?
   B: I'm from Laos.
   A: Please spell that for me.
   B: L-A-O-S.
   A: L-A-O-S. And what's your first language?
   B: Chinese.
   A: Chinese? Really?
   B: Yes, really. Do you want me to spell it?
   A: C-H-I-N-E-S-E, right?
   B: Sorry, I didn't catch that.
   A: C-H-I-N-E-S-E.
   B: Right.

Number.

1. A: Hi. I haven't seen you here before. Are you a new student?
   B: Yes, I am. I'm a little nervous.
   A: Don't worry. The teacher is nice. Where are you from?
   B: Laos.
   B: Laos? Where's that?
   A: It's between Thailand and Vietnam.

2. A: Hi. My name's Mei Le. You're Victor, aren't you?
   B: Yes, I am. Nice to meet you, Mei Le.
   A: Somebody said you're from Russia.
   B: Yes, that's right. I'm from Russia.
   A: What part of Russia?

B: I'm from Smolensk. It's in the west.

3. A: I heard they speak 16 different languages in your country. Is that true?
   B: Yes, it is.
   A: Well, how many languages do you speak?
   B: Me? Just Hindi.
   A: Is Hindi what most of the people speak?
   B: Most of them, yes.

4. A: You speak French, don't you?
   B: A little. I studied it in school for six years, but I don't speak it well.
   A: What's your first language, then?
   B: English.
   A: Oh! I thought you were a student here.
   B: No, I work in the office.

5. A: How do you say Monday in Portuguese?
   B: Sorry, I don't know.
   A: Don't you speak Portuguese?
   B: No, I don't.
   A: Oh, sorry. Where are you from, then?
   B: I'm from Egypt.
   A: Egypt! I thought you were from Brazil. My mistake.
   B: No problem.

Exercise 4. What about you?

Hi. I'm Donna Jones. I'm from Austin, Texas. What about you?

Exercise 1. What's next?

a.

1. A: How's your new apartment, Beth?
What's next?

2. A: Mr. Rogers, this is Mrs. Neal. Mrs. Neal, this is Mr. Rogers.
What's next?

3. A: I'm looking for a one-bedroom apartment. Do you have an apartment for rent?
   B: Yes, we do. Please have a seat.
What's next?

4. A: Hello. We're looking for an apartment.
   B: Please come in. I'm Jean Gillette.
   A: I'm Gary Morris.
What's next?

5. A: Call me tomorrow if you want the apartment. Here's my telephone number.
What's next?

6. A: We finally found an apartment. It's near my job and there's a good school for the children.
   B: Good. Do you like the apartment?

b.

1. A: Where is Shelley and Bernie's new house?
   B: It's across the street from the hospital.
   A: Oh! Do they live on the same street as Charles?
What's next?

124

2. A: You say the rent is $725 a month?
   B: That's right. And it includes utilities.
   A: Does it come with drapes and carpeting?
What's next?

3. A: Excuse me. Do you have a two-bedroom apartment for rent?
   B: Yes, I do. It's on the second floor in the back.
   A: Do you have any two-bedrooms in the front of the building?
What's next?

4. A: How many bedrooms do you need?
   B: Two. I need an extra bedroom for my grandchildren.
   A: Oh. Do your grandchildren visit you often?
What's next?

5. A: And the rent is $500 a month.
   B: Does the rent include utilities?
What's next?

6. A: Do you have a stove and refrigerator in the apartment?
   B: Yes, I do. They're brand new.
   A: That's great. Do you have a washer and dryer too?
What's next?

**Exercise 2. Review... Write... Number.
Write the rent and the security deposit.**

a. A: We're interested in the apartment. We like the appliances. We don't have a refrigerator or stove.
   B: Well, as I said, the appliances are only 2 years old.
   A: What did you say the rent was?
   B: The rent is $685.
   A: $685. And the deposit?
   B: One and a half months. That comes to $1,027.50.
   A: That's a lot.

b. A: So, are you interested in the apartment?
   B: Yes, we like it. The rooms are big and it seems to have enough closet space. Now, you said the rent was $540?
   A: Yes, that's right. And the deposit is only $300.
   B: When is it available?
   A: March 1st.
   B: Oh. That's a problem. We're getting married on February 14th.

c. A: This apartment is beautiful. And it's ready to move into immediately.
   B: Yes, but do we have to buy our own stove and refrigerator?
   A: Yes. You can get any kind you like. Just be sure they can fit in the space.
   B: And the rent is $735?
   A: That's correct. $735.
   B: And how much is the deposit?
   A: The deposit is two months' rent, $1,470.
   B: OK. Thanks. We'll let you know.

d. A: I really like the apartment. And I love the carpeting. It'll be perfect with my furniture.
   B: I'm glad you like it.
   A: Now, you said the rent was $625 a month?
   B: Yes, that's right. And the deposit is $937.50.
   A: OK. I'll think it over and call you tomorrow.

Number.

1. A: I like this room.

B: Me, too. The drapes are pretty, aren't they? And our new furniture would look nice here.
   A: Yes, the bed could go here and the dresser could go against that wall.
   B: Silvio, I like this apartment. Let's take it.
   A: I like it too, but let's wait. We have three more apartments to look at.

2. A: How do you like the kitchen?
   B: Well, it's nice and big. But it doesn't have a stove or refrigerator. We'd have to buy them.
   A: I know. And they're expensive. But we'd get the kind we like.
   B: Yes, but we can't afford the kind we'd like.
   A: You're right. Maybe this apartment is too expensive for us. The rent and deposit are more than $2,000, plus the appliances.
   B: Yeah. Let's forget about this one.

3. A: This is a nice room. And the closet is big.
   B: They always look big when they're empty.
   A: Seriously, Silvio. We can afford the rent here. And the deposit is low.
   B: I know. But remember, it doesn't have drapes or carpeting. We'd have to buy them.
   A: That's true.

4. A: What do you think?
   B: It's too small. We can't eat here. There's no space for a table.
   A: Um. But look at the appliances. The refrigerator looks new.
   B: So does the stove. And it's gas. I like that.
   A: So?
   B: I don't know. I still like the first apartment we saw.
   A: Me too.... Let's take it.

Exercise 4. What about you?

I live in an apartment. It has two bedrooms, a living room, and a kitchen. What about you?

UNIT 3   Page 32   Listening Plus.

Exercise 1. What's next?

a.
1. A: Hi, Sandra. Where are you going?
   B: To the DMV — the Department of Motor Vehicles.
   A: What for?
   B: I'm taking my road test today for my driver's license.
What's next?

2. A: Hey, Don. Do you want a ride home?
   B: Sure. Who's driving?
   A: I am. I got my license!
What's next?

3. A: What's the matter, Frances? You look upset.
   B: I *am* upset. I didn't pass the written test for my learner's permit. I guess I didn't study enough.
What's next?

4. A: Hi, Helen. How's your new apartment?
   B: Oh, hi, Ibrahim. I didn't get the apartment. Someone else got there first.
What's next?

5. A: Hey, Mike. Look what I got.
   B: What?

A: My learner's permit. Now I can drive!
What's next?

6. A: Have you moved into your new apartment yet?
   B: Oh, we didn't take that apartment. It was too expensive. But tomorrow we're going to look at another one. It sounds pretty good.
What's next?

b.
1. A: Where's Pablo today?
   B: He's looking for an apartment. He needs to move by next week.
   A: Oh, that's right. Does he want to live in town?
What's next?

2. A: Did you see Kim this morning?
   B: Yes, I did. She wasn't very happy.
   A: Did she pass her eye test?
What's next?

3. A: Level 1 had a different teacher last night.
   B: Really?
   A: Yes. His name's John.
   B: Oh, I know him. He's good. Did the students like him?
What's next?

4. A: Do you know where Sam lives?
   B: I think he lives on Madison Street.
   A: Does he live near the hospital?
What's next?

5. A: Margaret and Oscar are such a nice couple.
   B: Yes, they are. Everybody likes them.
   A: Did they study here last year too?
What's next?

6. A: Is Laura going to the post office?
   B: No. She went this morning.
   A: Oh. Did she get stamps?
What's next?

**Exercise 2. Review... Write... Number. Write.
Fill in the addresses. Use abbreviations.**

a. A: Joan, what's your new address?
   B: It's 222 South Wilson Street, Apartment 202, Mule Creek, New Mexico 88051.
   A: OK. What's the abbreviation for South?
   B: South? It's S. Just capital S, period.
   A: And for Apartment?
   B: Apartment is A-P-T period.
   A: And New Mexico?
   B: N-M.
   A: With periods?
   B: No, just the letters. N-M.
   A: So it's 222 South Wilson Street, Apt. 202, Mule Creek, New Mexico 88051. Thanks.

b. A: What's Marta's address?
   B: It's 1660 West Main Street, Apartment H, Fox Lake, Illinois.
   A: 1660 West Main Street. How do I write West? Just W.?
   B: The abbreviation? Yes, W period.
   A: And Main is M-A-I-N?
   B: That's right.
   A: OK. And what was the apartment again?
   B: H. 1660 West Main Street, Apartment H. Do you want the abbreviation for Illinois too?
   A: It's I-L, isn't it?
   B: That's right.

c. A: What's Tom's street address?
   B: Tom's? It's 1595 Utah Boulevard North.

A: Wait a minute. Is that U-T-A-H?
B: Uh-huh.
A: OK. Now how do I write the rest with abbreviations?
B: Boulevard is B-L-V-D period. North is capital N period.
A: 1595 Utah Boulevard North. Oh—one more question. He lives in Iowa City, Iowa. What's the abbreviation for the state? Is it I-O?
B: No. It's I-A.

d. A: Does Felix live on East Adams Street or West Adams Street?
B: East Adams Street. If you're writing it, you just need to write capital E, period, for East.
A: And is Adams with one D or two?
B: One. It's A-D-A-M-S. 222 East Adams Street.
A: And that's in Hartford, Connecticut?
B: Uh-huh.
A: How do you spell Connecticut?
B: Just write C-T. It's easier.
A: C-T. Thanks.

Number.

1. A: Bill, is this the money order for Mr. Hawkins?
B: Yes, it is.
A: This is just for seventy-five dollars. I thought we owed him a *hundred* and seventy-five dollars.
B: We did. I sent him a hundred last week.
A: Oh, good.... I see he's living in Iowa now. When did he move there?
B: Not long ago — last month.

2. A: Is this the money order for the furniture?
B: Yes.
A: Hum. Four hundred and fifty dollars is a good price. Do you want me to mail this for you?
B: No thanks. Dr. Randolph is going to be at our store in Hartford tomorrow. I'll just give it to him.

3. A: Joan, do you want me to mail these letters for you?
B: Yes, thanks. That would be great.
A: Hey, this one doesn't have a stamp.
B: Really? I thought I put stamps on all of them. Let me see.... Oh, that's the letter to Richard. You're right. Here's a stamp for it.

4. A: Do you still write to Marta?
B: Sure. In fact I was just going to the post office with a letter for her. See?
A: Uh-huh. What a pretty stamp.... I see she's living in Illinois now. How does she like it?
B: She says it's cold.

Exercise 4. What about you?

I live in Bridgeton, California, now. My house is on Jay Street. What about you?

UNIT 4   Page 44   Listening Plus.

Exercise 1. What's next?

a.

1. A: Ruth, your English is really good. How long did you study English?
What's next?

2. A: This is my daughter. That's her wedding picture.
B: She's really beautiful. When did she get married?

What's next?

3. A: Here's the enrollment form for Jamie Goldberg, Mr. Smith.
B: Wait a minute, Danny. What's his date of birth?
What's next?

4. A: I went to see Bettina's new house yesterday. It's really nice.
B: I didn't know she moved.
A: Yes. She lives in Norwood now.
B: When did she move?
What's next?

5. A: Elena, can you help me with this form? What do I put here?
B: Let's see. They want your date of arrival in the U.S.
A: The date I came here?
B: Yes.
What's next?

6. A: It's so *cold* today, just like Chicago.
B: Did you use to live in Chicago?
A: Uh-huh.
B: How long did you live there?
What's next?

b.

1. A: Where's Roger?
B: I don't think he came to class today.
A: Did he come last Friday?
What's next?

2. A: Where are your parents from?
B: They were born in Armenia.
A: Did they go to school in the U.S.?
What's next?

3. A: Martine, did Rose get her school ID yesterday?
What's next?

4. A: Tell me about Sam. Did he pass his test?
What's next?

5. A: Rosa and Tomas are good students, aren't they?
B: Yes, they're excellent.
A: Did they study English in Guatemala?
What's next?

Exercise 2. Review... Write... Number.
Write their dates of birth.

a. A: Please state your full name.
B: Margaret Freda Weiss Becker.
A: Where were you born, Mrs. Becker?
B: In Altenberg, Germany.
A: And when was that?
B: I was born on March 22, 1930.
A: Are you married?
B: I am a widow. My husband died in 1987.
A: I see. When did you come to the U.S.?
B: I came to live with my daughter Marlena and her family in 1990.

b. A: Miss Becker, we need a little more information here. Is *Ana* spelled with one *n* or two?
B: Just one, A-N-A.
A: Is this your current address?
B: Yes, it is.
A: And what's your date of birth?
B: October 15, 1957.
A: 10/15/57. Thank you. I think that's everything.

c. A: Is your name Marlena Becker?
B: That was my maiden name. My married name is Braun.
A: When did you get married?
B: In 1968.
A: When did you come to the U.S.?

B: My husband and I came in 1969.
A: What is your date of birth, Mrs. Braun?
B: I was born on September 1, 1950.
A: And you have three children?
B: Yes, I do.

d. A: You are Walter Braun?
B: That's correct.
A: Your wife is Marlena Becker Braun?
B: Yes.
A: Were you born in the United States?
B: No, I wasn't, but I became a U.S. citizen in 1975.
A: What is your date of birth?
B: December 26, 1946.
A: You have three children, I believe. Were they born in this country?
B: Yes, they were.
A: That's all. Thank you very much.

e. A: Ah, yes, Miss Braun. What's your first name, please?
B: Erica. I'm Erica Braun.
A: And what is your birth date, Miss Braun?
B: September 24, 1970.

f. A: Hello. Let's see.... You must be Steven Braun.
B: That's right.
A: And what's your date of birth, Mr. Braun?
B: December 1, 1972.
A: 12/1/72.
B: Right.

g. A: Freda Braun?
B: That's right.
A: When were you born, please?
B: July 27, 1974.
A: Excuse me? I didn't catch that.
B: July 27, 1974.
A: Thank you.

Number.

1. I'm Marlena's husband. I was born on December 26, 1946. Who am I?
2. My parents are Marlena and Walter. I was born in 1974. Who am I?
3. I'm Steven's and Freda's sister. My birthday is September 24, 1970. Who am I?
4. My sister has three children. I'm their aunt. Who am I?
5. I'm Marlena's mother. I came to the United States after my husband died. Who am I?
6. I am my parent's only son, but I have two sisters. Who am I?
7. I live with my mother, my husband, and my three children. Who am I?

Exercise 4. What about you?

I was born in Tokyo, Japan. I arrived in the United States on May 16, 1991. What about you?

UNIT 5   Page 56   Listening Plus.

Exercise 1. What's next?

a.

1. A: Are you OK?
B: No, I'm not. I have a headache, my back hurts, my neck hurts — everything hurts. I think I'm really sick.
A: You shouldn't go to work today. Do you want me to call your boss?
What's next?

2. A: What's wrong?
B: Ahmed Jamali's friend just phoned. Ahmed's in the hospital.
What's next?

3. A: Well, Mr. Chang, you have the flu. You need to stay in bed and rest for at least a week.
    B: But I have to go to work.
    A: You can't work. You're too sick. Take this letter and give it to your supervisor. If there's any problem, they can phone me.
    What's next?
4. A: I'm sorry I'm late. I was at the hospital.
    What's next?
5. A: There. Your foot is going to be OK, but you can't walk. You need crutches.
    B: How can I get home if I can't walk?
    A: Don't worry. We phoned your wife. She'll be here in a few minutes.
    What's next?
6. A: Hello?
    B: Mrs. Lee? I'm calling from the hospital. Your son is here in the emergency room. He had to get some stitches in his head.
    What's next?

b.
1. A: Mama just called. They're still at the doctor's office. There was some emergency and they haven't seen the doctor yet.
    B: But they have to be at work in 30 minutes. What are they going to do?
    What's next?
2. A: Mimi looks tired. What's the matter?
    B: The baby cried all night. She didn't sleep.
    A: What's she going to do?
    What's next?
3. A: Jim has a fever. He can't go to school today.
    B: What's he going to do all day?
    What's next?
4. A: Where's Dad?
    B: He's still sleeping. He had to work overtime last night.
    A: What's he going to do today?
    What's next?
5. A: Did Grandma come back from the doctor's office?
    B: Yes, she did.
    A: Is she OK?
    B: Yes, she's fine, but she's tired.
    A: What's she going to do this afternoon?
    What's next?
6. A: Carlos and Felipe missed the train.
    B: When do you think they'll get here?
    What's next?

Exercise 2. Review... Write... Number.
Write the treatments you hear.

a. A: Hello?
    B: Hello, Indy. Listen, the baby's OK.
    A: Oh, that's great. I was so worried. Are you coming home now?
    B: Yes, we're going straight home. Do we have any children's aspirin in the house? That's all the baby needs.
    A: Yes, we have some children's aspirin in the medicine cabinet.
    B: That's fine. See you soon.
b. A: Hello?
    B: Hello. Mrs. Sanchez? This is Larry. Carlos had an accident.
    A: Oh, no! What happened? Is he all right?
    B: Don't worry. He's going to be OK. He burned his foot at work.
    A: Where is he now?

B: We're at the emergency room. I'm going to take him home now. We just have to stop and get a prescription. He needs some pain medicine so he can sleep.
c. A: Hello?
    B: Hello, dear. It's Mom.
    A: Oh, Mom. I've been worried. How is Kate?
    B: She's going to be fine. She needed stitches, but it's nothing dangerous. We'll be home soon.
    A: OK, Mom. Thanks for calling.
d. A: Hello?
    B: Mom. Grandpa's all right. It wasn't a heart attack. It was just his stomach.
    A: Oh.... I was so worried.
    B: I know. He still has a lot of pain, but he just needs some antacid. The doctor gave him a prescription.
    A: OK. Are you coming home now?
    B: Yes. We'll be there in twenty minutes.
e. A: Hello?
    B: Hello, Randy. Listen, can you pick up Nancy after school today?
    A: OK. Is anything wrong?
    B: Well, Willie fell off his bike and hurt his knee and I brought him to the emergency room.
    A: The emergency room!
    B: Yes, but don't worry. It's not so bad. He just needed a bandage.
    A: Good. How's he feeling?
    B: He's OK now.
f. A: Hello?
    B: Nick, this is Sally. Listen, Rick and I had an accident. I'm OK, but Rick needs X-rays. We're at the emergency room now.
    A: Is it serious?
    B: No. They say he might have a broken rib, but he's going to be fine.

Number.

1. Rick drove through a red light and hit another car. His sister was with him. She wasn't hurt, but Rick has a lot of cuts and bruises and he probably broke some bones. The doctor ordered X-rays. Now Rick is waiting to go to the X-ray department.
2. Mr. Oh went to the emergency room because he thought he was having a heart attack. He was lucky. He only had a bad stomachache. The doctor gave him a prescription for antacid and told him to go home. Mr. Oh was very relieved.
3. Rashid's baby boy had a fever. The baby was very hot and he cried all the time. Rashid and his wife were worried, but the doctor said it wasn't dangerous. They're going to give him children's aspirin to control the fever.
4. Willie was practicing tricks on his bike when he fell off and skinned his knee. His mother was afraid he had hurt himself badly, so she took him to the emergency room. Luckily, Willie wasn't hurt badly. And he didn't cry at all when the doctor cleaned his knee and bandaged it.
5. Kate likes to cook, and she's usually very careful in the kitchen, but today she cut her finger while she was cutting onions for a stew. The cut was very deep. Kate's mother couldn't stop the bleeding, so she took Kate to the emergency room to get stitches. Kate was scared, but she's feeling better now.

6. Carlos is a cook in a restaurant. A big pot of soup fell off the stove and burned his foot. He's in a lot of pain and he needs help to walk. His friend from work brought him to the emergency room and is going to take him home. Carlos will need to take something for the pain in order to sleep tonight.

Exercise 4. What about you?

When I get the flu, I don't go to school. I stay in bed and rest. What about you? What do you do for the flu?

UNIT 6   Page 68   Listening Plus.
Exercise 1. What's next?

a.
1. A: May I help you?
    B: Yes. I'd like three cans of tuna fish, please.
    What's next?
2. A: Who's next?
    B: I am. I'd like some of that cheese, please.
    What's next?
3. A: Boy, you bought a lot of food!
    B: I know. And I spent a lot of money!
    What's next?
4. A: Yes, sir, what can I get you?
    B: Two barbecued chickens, please.
    What's next?

b.
1. A: I don't have enough rice. Will you get some for me at the supermarket?
    B: How many bags?
    What's next?
2. A: I'd like some ground beef. I'm making taco salad tonight.
    B: How much ground beef do you want?
    What's next?
3. A: Gloria is coming to dinner tonight. I'll need some more bread.
    B: How many loaves do you want?
    What's next?
4. A: I'm going to the supermarket. Do you want anything?
    B: I need some cheese.
    A: How much?
    What's next?

Exercise 2. Review... Write... Number.
Write the prices.

a. A: Wait a minute, dear. We need some rice.
    B: OK. There's the brand we like.
    A: What size do we usually get?
    B: Get the one-pound box. It should be 89¢.
    A: Yes, you're right. It is.
b. A: Who's next, please?
    B: I am. A pound of Swiss cheese, please.
    A: Imported or domestic?
    B: How much is the imported?
    A: $4.99 a pound.
    B: OK. I'll take a pound.
c. A: Do you want a bottle or can? The apple juice comes in both.
    B: A can. One quart is good.
    A: It's 99¢.
    B: That's what it usually is.
    A: Should I get two?
    B: No, just one is enough.
d. A: This rice is on sale.
    B: How much is it?
    A: Five pounds for $2.99.

B: That's great. It should last a month.
A: Not in my house! I'll be lucky if it lasts two weeks.

e. A: Is apple juice on the list?
B: Yes. We need a gallon.
A: Is this the brand your mother usually buys?
B: Let me see. Yes, that's it, Dad.
A: Hmm. It's on special this week — $2.19.

f. A: May I help you?
B: Yes. I'm having a party and I need some cheese. What do you recommend?
A: Here's a very nice yellow cheese. How many people are you having?
B: About 30. And I'm having other things.
A: I think you need about five pounds.
B: And how much is it?
A: $2.29 a pound.

g. A: I can't find the grated cheese.
B: I think they keep it with the spaghetti and sauces.
A: You're right. Here it is.
B: Here's an eight ounce jar. Is this enough?
A: Yeah, I think so. How much is it?
B: It's $1.29.

h. A: I really like this apple juice, Terry.
B: Me, too. Do you see a larger size?
A: No, just these eight ounce bottles.
B: Get a few. How much are they?
A: 89¢ a piece.
B: Wow, that's a lot.

i. A: Sally, can you hand me that box of rice, please?
B: Which one?
A: The two-pound box.
B: I didn't even see this! Hey, this is a good buy.
A: Why? How much is it?
B: $1.89. I saw the same thing at Foodsmart for 30¢ more.

Number.

1. A: Excuse me. There's no price on this.
B: Sorry, sir. That's $2.19 a gallon.
A: Thanks.
B: You bet.

2. A: Excuse me. Is this the one on sale?
B: No, ma'am. That would be the two-pound box. Right over here.
A: Thank you.
B: You're very welcome.

3. A: May I help you?
B: Yes. Is this the regular price?
A: No, sir. It's the sale price. $4.99 a pound. This week only. Would you like some?
B: Let me think about it.
A: Sure. No problem.

4. A: Pardon me. Can you please reach that box for me?
B: Sure, miss. Which one?
A: The one-pound box. Thanks.

5. A: Hey, Bill, there are no prices on these cans.
B: Are you sure?
A: Sure, I'm sure. Look. Does this can have a price on it?
B: Sure, it does. It's right there on the side.
A: Whoops! Sorry, I missed it.

6. A: Price check. I need a price check.
B: Hold it up higher, please. I can't see.
A: It's the eight ounce jar.
B: OK. Just a minute.

7. A: Would you put this stuff back on the shelf, please?
B: Sure. Where does the rice go?
A: The five pound size goes on the bottom shelf.

8. A: Get some apple juice for a change, OK?
B: But nobody likes it.
A: *I* like it. Just get some of the eight ounce size.

9. A: That's too much cheese.
B: The man said five pounds was good for thirty people.
A: Well, let's hope they finish it.

Exercise 4. What about you?

I drink coffee, my husband drinks tea, and the baby drinks milk. What about your family?

UNIT 7   Page 80   Listening Plus.

Exercise 1. What's next?

a.

1. A: Do you have any job openings for cooks?
B: Yes, we do. But you need to have experience.
A: I have experience. I was a fry cook for six months.
B: Can you work full time?
What's next?

2. A: Here's my application form for the sewing job.
B: Ms. Jones will be right with you. Please have a seat.
What's next?

3. A: Janet, here's an ad for factory workers.
B: What kind of work?
A: Assembly. And it pays $5.75 an hour. Uh-oh. It's night shift only. Night shift is OK for me. Can you work night shift?
What's next?

4. A: Do you have any openings for mechanics?
B: Yes, we're looking for two mechanics right now. Do you want to fill out an application?
A: Yes, please.
B: OK. Here. And bring it back to me when you finish.
What's next?

b.

1. A: A friend of mine is looking for a job.
B: Did she fill out an application?
A: Yes, she did.
B: We have an opening on the late shift. Can she work nights?
What's next?

2. A: Hey, Ruth. Have you seen Roberta tonight?
B: No, I haven't. I guess she's out. Was she here last night?
What's next?

3. A: Dora's out sick tonight. I need a driver for her truck.
B: What about Pete? Can he drive it?
What's next?

4. A: I can't come to work on Thursday morning next week. I have a doctor's appointment.
B: Maybe Ginger can take over for you. Can she work on Thursdays?
What's next?

5. A: When did Roy start to work here?
B: I don't remember. The new factory opened in 1989. Was he here then?
What's next?

6. A: Marlene, there's an opening for a driver where I work. Does your husband have any job experience driving?
B: No, but he's a good driver.
A: Can he drive a van?
What's next?

Exercise 2. Review... Write... Number. Write the pay and the hours you hear.

a. A: Hello. I'd like to get some information about your assembly job.
B: OK. What do you want to know?
A: What shifts are available?
B: Just the late shift, 11:30 p.m. to 7:30 a.m.
A: And what's the salary, please?
B: $6.35 an hour.
A: Okay. Full-time, late shift, $6.35 an hour.
B: That's right.
A: Thank you.

b. A: Hello. Do you still have a job opening for a baker?
B: Yes, we do.
A: Can you tell me the hourly wage?
B: It's $8.50 an hour if you have experience.
A: And what are the hours?
B: 4:00 a.m. to 12 noon, four days a week.
A: I see. Thanks.

c. A: What are the hours for the sewing job, please?
B: We have openings in our second shift, 3:30 p.m. to 11:30 p.m. You have half an hour for lunch, and two 15 minute breaks.
A: And what do you pay per hour?
B: We start at $4.25.
A: Thank you.

d. A: Hello. I'd like some information about your delivery job. Is the job still available?
B: Yes, but just on the weekends.
A: Oh. Well, what are the hours?
B: Friday and Saturday, 4:00 p.m. to 12:00 midnight.
A: I know there are tips, but what do you pay per hour?
B: We pay $3.75.
A: Thanks very much.

e. A: Do I need any experience for the janitor's job?
B: No, we'll train you on the job.
A: What are the hours?
B: 6:00 p.m. to 2:00 a.m.
A: That's really late. Well, how about the pay?
B: We pay $4.50 an hour to start, with a raise and benefits in four weeks.
A: OK. Thanks.

f. A: Are you the company with the ad for cashiers?
B: That's right. The job's in our downtown parking garage.
A: What are the hours, please?
B: 6:00 a.m. to 2:00 p.m., weekdays.
A: And what do you pay?
B: We start at $4.50 an hour.
A: Thanks.

Number.

1. A: How about this job?
B: But it's only part-time.
A: That's true, but it's four days a week — and it pays $8.50 an hour!

2. A: Do you like to drive?
   B: Sure. Is there a driving job in the paper?
   A: Yes. It's a delivery job.
   B: But I don't have a car.
   A: That's OK. The ad says they have a car. And you get tips too.
3. A: Here's a notice for a cashier.
   B: What are the hours?
   A: Early shift, 6:00 a.m. to 2:00 p.m.
   B: That sounds good. I'll call about that one.
4. A: Here's a job. I don't think they want experience.
   B: Oh, good. Is it full-time or part-time?
   A: Full-time. But the hours are terrible — 11:30 at night to 7:30 in the morning.
5. A: Do you see any job notices for sewing?
   B: Yeah, here's one.
   A: What does it pay?
   B: Four and a quarter an hour.
6. A: Here are some jobs we could apply for. Look at this notice.
   B: Let me see. Well, that's good. We don't need experience.
   A: No. And we'd get benefits.
   B: Uh-huh. The pay's not great, but you get a raise in four weeks.
   A: Sounds good. Let's go!

Exercise 4. What about you?

My first job was burger cook at Hamburger Heaven. It was a part-time job. What about you? What was your first job?

UNIT 8 Page 92 Listening Plus.

Exercise 1. What's next?

a.
1. A: Roger, do you still have the tape measure?
   B: No. I put it on the top shelf.
   A: But it goes on the bottom shelf.
What's next?
2. A: Can I speak to you for a minute, please?
   B: Sure. What's up?
   A: I need to leave a few minutes early today. Is that all right?
What's next?
3. A: Hey, James, do you have the screwdriver?
   B: No, I don't. Ask Scott.
What's next?
4. A: I can't find my hammer. Do you know where it is?
   B: I'm not sure, but I saw it yesterday. It was on the pegboard.
What's next?
5. A: I'd like to cash my paycheck, please.
   B: Certainly, ma'am. Uh, excuse me, but you didn't endorse it.
What's next?
6. A: Do you have the flashlight?
   B: The flashlight? No. Didn't I give it back to you?
What's next?

b.
1. A: John, I can't find anything today.
   B: What are you looking for? Maybe I know.
   A: Where is the extension cord?
What's next?

2. A: Oh, Dora, have you seen Bill or my sister? We had an appointment at the hospital.
   B: Bill just left a few minutes ago.
   A: And my sister?
What's next?
3. A: You've made quite a mess here!
   B: I know. I just need to cut the thread from the machine and start over again. Where are the scissors?
What's next?
4. A: Where are Antonio and John?
   B: I guess they're at work.
   A: Already? How did they get there?
What's next?
5. A: Are the tools over there, by you?
   B: No.
   A: Well, do you know where the wrench is?
What's next?
6. A: The buses were all running late this morning.
   B: Well, Betty got to work on time.
   A: How?
What's next?

Exercise 2. Review... Write... Number.
Write the names of the tools in the right places.

a. A: Do you have the hammer?
   B: The hammer? No, but I saw it a minute ago.
   A: Oh, there it is, on the top shelf to the right of the scissors.
b. A: Now, where did I put the tape measure? It's not on the table and it's not on the shelves.
   B: There it is. It must have fallen. It's on the floor under the table.
   A: Oh, thanks.
c. A: Would you hand me the pliers, please?
   B: The what?
   A: The pliers.
   B: Where are they?
   A: They're on the table, to the left of the screwdriver.
d. A: George wants the wrench.
   B: The adjustable wrench?
   A: Yes.
   B: OK. Why don't you get it for him? It's on the bottom shelf, next to the extension cord.
e. A: Have you seen the saw? I've looked everywhere.
   B: It's over there — on the wastebasket.
   A: No wonder I couldn't see it. That's not where it belongs.
f. A: I need the nails. Do you know where they are?
   B: The nails or the screws?
   A: The nails, I said. Where did you put them?
   B: They're on the middle shelf, right where they belong.

Number.
Write numbers next to the words.

1. They're on the table. They're to the left of the screwdriver.
2. It's to the right of the table. The saw is on it.
3. They're on a shelf. They're not on the bottom shelf. They're not on the middle shelf.
4. They're on the corner of the table. They're to the right of the screwdriver.

5. It's not on the table. It's not on the floor. It's not on the wastebasket. It's not on the top shelf. It's not on the middle shelf. It's not the wrench.
6. It's not on the table. It's not on the floor. It's not on the wastebasket. It's not on the bottom shelf. It's not on the middle shelf.

Exercise 4. What about you?

I was late for work one day last week. I waited and waited, but the bus didn't come. What about you? Were you ever late?

UNIT 9 Page 104 Listening Plus.

Exercise 1. What's next?

a.
1. A: Here are your purchases. Have a nice day.
   B: Thank you. The same to you.
   A: Wait. I forgot to give you a shopping bag. Here you are. Sorry.
What's next?
2. A: Good afternoon. May I help you?
   B: Yes, thanks. Do you have these pants in yellow?
What's next?
3. A: Here's your change. That's $2.34.
   B: Excuse me. I gave you a twenty. My change should be $12.34.
What's next?
4. A: Excuse me. These shoes are too tight. Do you have them in a size 8?
What's next?
5. A: I'm sorry, ma'am, but we're out of that color right now.
What's next?
6. B: So, did that sweater fit?
   A: No, it didn't. I need a medium, but you gave me a large.
What's next?

b.
1. A: Come on out, Alex. How do you like the sweats?
   B: I really like them, Dad. But do they fit OK?
What's next?
2. A: Marta, you've got to see the new skirt I bought.
   B: It's great. Try it on. Let me see.
   A: OK.... What do you think?
What's next?
3. A: Excuse me.
   B: Yes? May I help you?
   A: Yes. I'd like to try on this jacket, but I need a small.
   B: That *is* a small.
What's next?
4. A: How do those pants fit?
   B: See for yourself. They feel really comfortable. Do you like them?
What's next?

Exercise 2. Review... Write... Number.
Write the prices on the price tags.

a. A: Excuse me. Can I see this sweater in a medium?
   B: Certainly. Here you are.
   A: Thanks. How much is it?
   B: It's $44.00. A real bargain.
b. A: I need a gift for my brother. How much is that black sweater?

B: It's $14.00. Would you like to see it?
A: Yes, please, in a small.
B: Let me see if I have any smalls.

c. A: I think I'll get my father this cardigan for his birthday.
B: Does he like sweaters?
A: Yes, as long as they don't itch. He wears a large. I hope they have one.
B: How much is it?
A: It's $40.00.

d. A: That dress is perfect on you. What size is it?
B: It's size 12. Are you sure my knees don't look funny?
A: Your knees look fine. You have great legs.
B: Thanks. It's a good buy. It's only $39.95.
A: Hey, that's great.

e. A: What do you think of this dress?
B: Are you sure it's not too long?
A: Positive. This is the way it's supposed to look. It's a size 2 and I always wear a size 2.
B: OK. Whatever you say. How much is it?
A: Just $30.95.
B: Not bad.

f. A: Excuse me, miss. I need a dress for a cocktail party.
B: How about this one? The colors are right for you.
A: OK. Can I see it in size 20?
B: Sure. I'll be right back.
A: By the way, is it on sale?
B: Yes, it is. It's $139.95.
A: Oh.

Number.

1. It's smaller than the white sweater and larger than the black sweater.
2. It's longer than the checked dress and shorter than the print dress.
3. It's larger than the striped sweater and larger than the black sweater.
4. It's shorter than the yellow dress and shorter than the print dress.
5. It's smaller than the white sweater and smaller than the yellow-and-white sweater.
6. It's longer than the size 12 dress and longer than the size 2 dress.

Exercise 4. What about you?

Right now, I'm wearing blue jeans, a striped shirt, and sneakers. I'm not wearing a jacket today. What about you?

UNIT 10 Page 116 Listening Plus.

Exercise 1. What's next?

a.

1. A: Are you going somewhere this summer, Alice?
B: No, not this year. But in August my sisters are coming to visit.
What's next?

2. A: Good-bye, everyone. I'll send you a postcard from Paris. See you in two weeks.
What's next?

3. A: Welcome back. How was the wedding?
B: It was beautiful!

A: And how was the trip home?
B: Well, our plane got in at 2:00 in the morning.
A: That's terrible. How do you feel?
What's next?

4. A: Are you ready to go?
B: Yes. In fact, there's my bus.
What's next?

5. A: What's new, Jesse?
B: My son and his family are coming to visit us from Chicago.
What's next?

6. A: Hi. It's good to see you. You've been away for a long time.
B: Yes, for three months.
A: That's a long time to travel. Aren't you tired?
What's next?

b.

1. A: When you came to the U.S., did you fly?
B: Yes. It was my first plane trip.
A: And when did you come?
What's next?

2. A: What time do we need to get there?
B: Early. Maybe 6:00.
A: How long will the trip take?
What's next?

3. A: Let's take the bus together tomorrow.
B: OK. What time do you usually leave?
What's next?

4. A: I'm leaving early today. I have to meet my mother at the airport. She's coming for the weekend.
B: That's nice. She lives in San Francisco, doesn't she?
A: Uh-huh.
B: How long is the flight from there?
What's next?

5. A: Hurry up, Don. We're going to be late.
B: I'm coming, I'm coming. When does the movie start, anyway?
What's next?

6. A: So when you came to the United States, first you went to Hong Kong?
B: Yes. I was lucky. I had relatives there.
A: That was lucky. When did you leave Hong Kong?
What's next?

Exercise 2. Review... Write... Number
Write departure and arrival times, with a.m. or p.m.

a. Bus number 3 for New York City is boarding at gate 6. It will depart at 7:30 a.m. and arrive in New York City at 9:55 p.m. All passengers for New York City, your bus is leaving from gate 6, with departure at 7:30 and arrival in New York at 9:55 p.m.

b. Attention, please. Flight 162 to New York LaGuardia airport is now boarding at Gate 26 for departure at 6:00. Estimated time of arrival in New York is 11:55 a.m. Flight 162 to New York is now boarding at Gate 26 for departure at 6:00 a.m. Estimated time of arrival in New York LaGuardia is 11:55 a.m. Immediate boarding, please.

c. All aboard, Amtrak passengers for Los Angeles. Boarding has begun for Amtrak service to Los Angeles, California. Scheduled departure time is 7:30 a.m., with

arrival in Los Angeles at 9:55 a.m. All aboard, Amtrak service to Los Angeles will depart at 7:30 a.m., with arrival in Los Angeles at 9:55 a.m. All aboard!

d. May I have your attention. The bus for St. Louis is now boarding at Gate 13, with departure at 6:00 and arrival in St. Louis at 11:55 p.m. Attention, all passengers for St. Louis. Your bus is boarding now. The St. Louis bus departs at 6:00 p.m. and arrives in St. Louis at 11:55.

e. Attention, travellers on Flight 729 for Denver, we have immediate boarding at Gate 28. Flight 729 will depart at 7:00 a.m. with arrival in Denver scheduled for 8:30 a.m. Flight 729 for Denver is now boarding at Gate 28, with departure at 7:00 a.m. and scheduled arrival at 8:30 a.m.

f. Attention. Attention, all passengers for Amtrak service to Denver. Now boarding at Gate 3, with departure at 7:00 p.m. Scheduled arrival in Denver is 8:30 this evening. All aboard for Amtrak service to Denver, Colorado. We are boarding at Gate 3, and departing at 7:00 p.m., with arrival at 8:30 p.m. All aboard! All aboard!

Number.

1. A: How are you getting to New York? Are you going to drive?
B: No, not this time. You don't need a car in New York. I'm going to fly.
A: That's a good idea. How long is your flight?
B: About six hours.

2. A: And what time would you like to leave?
B: Well, my meeting is at 11:00. I'd like to arrive around 10:00.
A: We have a train leaving at 7:30 a.m., which arrives at 9:55 a.m.
B: That's perfect.

3. A: What time are you getting there?
B: We get in at 11:55, if we're on time.
A: 11:55 at *night*? Why so late?
B: Because I can't leave work early. This way I leave work at 5:00 and the bus leaves at 6:00.

4. A: When are you leaving for Denver?
B: Tomorrow morning at 7:00. I have to leave for the airport at 5:30.
A: That's really early.
B: Yes, but I'll arrive at 8:30 and have plenty of time to get to my interview.

5. A: How are you getting there?
B: By bus.
A: That's a long trip by bus.
B: Yes. It's more than 14 hours.

6. A: What are you going to do in Denver?
B: My sister's getting married. I'm going to be in the wedding.
A: That's nice. And you're taking the train?
B: Yes. It's a beautiful trip. Have you ever done it?
A: No, but I'd like to.

Exercise 4. What about you?

Last week, I drove to school, I walked to the store, and I took the bus to work. I didn't fly and I didn't take the train. What about you?

Basic Conversations

for Progress Checks: *What are the people saying?*

UNIT 1

3. A: Write *chalk*.
   B: How do you spell that?
   A: C-H-A-L-K.

4. A: Hello/Hi.
      I'm Frank/My name is Frank.
   B: Hello/Hi.
      I'm Le/My name is Le.

   A: Le, this is Lynn. Lynn this is Le.
   B: Glad/Nice to meet you.
   C: Glad/Nice to meet you too.

   C: Where are you from?
   B: I'm from California.

   A: Good night/bye.
   B: See you/See you Tuesday.

UNIT 2

1. A: Do you have an apartment for rent?
   B: Yes, I do.
   A: How many rooms does it have?
   B: Three. A bedroom, a living room, and a kitchen.
   A: What's the rent?
   B: $650.
   A: And what's the deposit?
   B: $1300.
   A: Does the rent include utilities?
   B: Yes. It includes water, gas, and electricity.

2. A: Where's the supermarket?
   B: It's on the next block.

UNIT 3

There are no conversations in these
Progress Checks.

UNIT 4

3. A: Where are you from?
   B: I'm from Mexico.
   A: How long did you go to school in Mexico?
   B: I went to school for six years.
   A: How long did you study English?
   B: I didn't study English.
   A: When did you arrive in the United States?
   B: On June 1, 1982.
   A: When did you enroll in your adult school?
   B: Four months ago.

UNIT 5

4. A: Stay in bed and rest/Stay home and rest.
   B: Stay in bed and rest?/Stay home and rest?
   A: Yes.

UNIT 6

2. A: I don't like oranges. I like apples.

3. A: We're going to the drugstore. Do you need
      anything?
   B: No, thank you.
   A: We're going to the supermarket, too. Do you need
      any milk?
   B: Yes, thanks. I need two quarts of milk.

4. A: She wants two quarts of milk.
   B: How many quarts?
   A: Two.

UNIT 7

2. A: Do you have any openings for factory workers?
   B: Yes, we do.

   A: Can you come for an interview tomorrow afternoon?
   B: I'm sorry. I can't. Can I come in the morning?
   B: Yes. Come at 10:00.

3. A: What job are you applying for?
   B: Cashier.
   A: Do you have any experience?
   B: Yes. I was a cashier in Mexico.
   A: Can you work full-time?
   B: No, part-time.
   A: What hours can you work?
   B: From 4:00 p.m. to 8:00 p.m.
   A: When can you start?
   B: Next Monday.

UNIT 8

2. A: Can you cash this check, please?
   B: Do you have any identification?
   A: Yes. Here's my driver's license.
   B: Thank you.

3. A: Where were you yesterday?
   B: I was sick.

4. A: I need the hammer. Did you put it away?
   B: Sorry. I forgot.

5. A: Put the dictionary on the desk. Put the pencil to the right of the dictionary.

UNIT 9

2. A: Do you have this sweater in small?
   B: Let me check.

3. A: He isn't tall and he isn't short. He has blond hair and brown eyes. He's wearing a jacket.
   B: It's Boris!

4. A: That comes to $22.00. Is that cash or charge?
   B: Cash.
   A: Here's your change.
   B: Excuse me. I gave you $40.00. My change should be $18.00.
   A: I'm sorry. Here you are.
   B: That's OK. No problem.

UNIT 10

2. A: What time does the Denver plane leave, please?
   B: 11:00 a.m.
   A: And what time does it get there?
   B: 1:00 p.m.

3. A: I'd like a ticket to Denver, please.
   B: One-way or round-trip?
   A: One-way. How much is it?
   B: $149.00.

4. A: When did you come to the United States?
   B: In 1987.
   A: How did you get here?
   B: I took the bus to Lima. Then I flew to Los Angeles.